Jamie's Joy

Honoring Grief, Creating Legacy, Celebrating Life

"Becuz' God Made Me That Way!"

Jamie Morgan Mychael Bratton-McNeeley
May 24, 1996 – April 24, 2002

Elene Y. F. Bratton
M.S., LMFT

DEDICATION

To all the ancestors and loved ones who have left their bodies too soon.

To my parents, Milton Carroll Bratton and Sandra Louise Pestov Bratton. Without them Jamie and Danielle would never exist. To the best dad in the whole wide world, Jamie's dad, Mychael McNeeley. To Jamie's auntie, my sister, Annie. To Jamie's sissy, Danielle Dellosa. To Jamie's God mom, Julie Kyker. To my daughter in love, and Jamie's auntie, Chelees Turner.

To the next generation (in order of birth):
Ashani Samea Riley (in Spirit with Jamie), Raell Jamie Devon Dellosa, Isaiah Jamie Dellosa, Destiny Ashani Cheri Dellosa, Jake Kryee Chapman and all those little people who call me "Grammy," with whom I have EVER interacted as a loving grand.

From here, there are just so many. My greatest fear is knowing that I will miss somebody, and they will not know what they mean to me.

From the very first moments of this most horrific experience, there have been those who have stepped up to support us to make sure we survived, with all the twists and turns life has taken, who have continued to help us heal and provide love and support to Jamie and Jamie's Joy. These are just the ones I know of and can remember before this goes to print; I am sure there have been many, many more—both seen and unseen, known and unknown.

Please know this list is in order of memory and flowing in some sequence of the event, not in order of importance:

Our first responders, whose names I will never know, words cannot express the gratitude I have for you to this very day, and I wish you healing and wellness in the face of such tragedy that you deal with daily. Reverend Blair Tabor (who visited regularly in our home with me and continued to provide sage Spiritual counsel), and Julie Kyker—who both went from hospital to hospital with us that first, fatal night.

Dr. Kathryn Dixon, Ellen Sheehan-Bruton, Mimi Goodman, Ruth Duke and Richard Conklin—who came to see me the day after we got the news, and an extra shout out to Richard who, in true social worker form, brought resources into our home (EAP-grief support, etc.). David McNeely—who, despite his phobic fear of flying, flew across the country with his wife Karen Bozman (Jamie's aunt), along with their young son Ari (Jamie's cousin), to support us in the early days; Rev. Gretchen Pena—who quilted a blanket from Jamie's clothes—and all the many people who supported us from Christ Church Unity—making a Sponge Bob-themed party for the kids at the service and bringing endless casseroles to our home, who allowed us to set up Jamie's Joy originally under the umbrella of the church.

Shelly Best—who drove down to San Diego from Santa Barbara for countless weeks to hold us and let us sob; Amber Hughes, Angela Bratton, Melanie Goodyear, Erica Forman (left her body in 2007), Alex Bratton, Julie Kyker, Tony Torres, Michelle Tyler, Ken Harrison, Sherry Shopoff, Roy Bowman, Calvin T. ("CT") Smith,

Rebecca Galdston, Darren Burke, Jonathan ("Jono") Smith (left his body in 2019), Brenda A., Frances L., Joan Bleu, Tawny Weir, Cheryl Ann Harrison—who all encircled us with love and became the basis of the Jamie's Joy steering committee, volunteers and supporters.

Karl Anthony and Jeanne Ligorio—who supported us with visits and song in our home ("Kral Antie," as Jamie called him, shared experiences and even wrote songs for Jamie, giving us such a comfort in those early days); Scott Kalechstein, Mark Stanton Welch, Joyce and Barry Vissel, Alan Cohen, who all gave us support through song and sage wisdom.

Dr. Ken Druck, Azim Khamisa, whose stories of courage and healing from their own losses inspired us, gave us courage to go on and places to share our grief with other similarly afflicted souls.

The Jenna Druck Foundation, the Compassionate Friends, Elizabeth and Sharp Hospice, Hospice of North Coast and Sharp Grief Camps.

Sherry Hulstine—who provided psychological safety and processing for our intense grief; Joan and Rolland Bleu—who spent hours connecting with Jamie through meditations and shared their visions of our boy in his new life.

Many local San Diego political leaders—who saw Jamie for the young community person that he was and supported us through coming to events, providing recognition of our work and approving the park and street name change. To SEIU Local 221 that was a big support in our annual events.

To my awesome neighborhood and our fabulous neighbors Linda Pennington, Tom Lashbrook and Larry May—and all the "Azalea Parksters" who banded together to dedicate benches around Azalea Park in honor of Jamie, the City Heights Area Planning Committee, and the San Diego City Council members Tony Atkins, Donna Fry, Charles Bowman III—and all those who helped us get a street named after Jamie, "Jamie's Way," in the place where he was raised, Azalea Park.

To the many, many parents we met and spoke to in person, over the phone and in support groups—especially those who had children pass—and the thousands and thousands of people who sent cards and prayers, letters and donations, went to Jamie's Joy events, got to know Jamie at the website, even without ever meeting him in his body, and supported us on this long climb out of acute grief, and allowed us to heal some skin after our souls were rubbed off, offered us space to find healing and who continue to care for us during this lifelong journey of loss.

Another shout out to: Shelly Best, Amber Hughes, Angela Bratton, Julie Kyker, Ronda Shelly (left her body in 2018), Ellen Bruton, Danielle Dellosa, Antonio Torres and Melanie Goodyear, Chelees Turner and many others who, for many years, formed the steering committee for Jamie's Joy, helping to plan, organize, market, secure donations, execute and work Jamie's Joy events and keep Jamie's spirit of Love*Joy*Peace*Connection alive in themselves and the world.

An additional shout out to my family that has never forgotten Jamie, who have raised their kids, my grands, to know their uncle by name and face, who have a relationship with him through our stories, our love and by our continuing to honor his legacy. I am so grateful to each of you, and so blessed to have you in my life. And to Lyric Hinojosa, one of Jamie's best friends growing up who, out of their friendship, love and remembering first got a tattoo of Jamie on her shoulder, then named her baby "James" in his honor. How can you not heal with love and support like this?

⌒•⌒

They say it takes a village to raise a child. I say it takes an even bigger village to support the family that's lost a child. All of those I've mentioned, and so many more humans and their supportive resources, organized processes and hard-won internal wisdoms, are the reason I can write this book:

Together you gave me room, tools, space, compassion and acceptance to heal and learn to live beside the loss of Jamie, allowing me to arrive in this place where I am now living my own life again, telling my story, with Jamie as an ever-present part of my life, instead of as I first was, living Jamie's life, where I was only a shadow of myself.

And, lastly, to Lisa the Dragon Lady of Editing, who believed in my story and has read every word, helping me to tell my truth.

Thank you all for this gift of love and healing.

⌒•⌒

CONTENTS

FOREWORD

I met Elene Bratton in 1991 at the "Whole Being Weekend," a retreat that happened each fall in the mountains of San Diego County. It was like nothing I had ever been to, with a wide variety of classes, groups, dancing, music, pitch-black night time hikes, and vegetarian food prepared and served communally. I was in a particularly expansive period of my life, learning all kinds of new concepts and ideas, spiritually open, my mind clear and flexible for perhaps the first time since I was a child. I formed some new friendships that I cherish to this day.

The first time I saw Elene, she was dancing at the Karl Anthony concert. It was a dimly lit room, and she appeared to be in a state of deep peace and joy as she swayed gracefully on the dance floor, alone but with others, eyes closed and face smiling. I was entranced by her, and by the energy of the weekend. She had something emanating from within that drew me to want to know more. I had no intention of meeting anyone or becoming involved romantically at the time, but it happened anyway, at least on my side. It took Elene longer to be "into" me, but we eventually started seeing each other, and moved in together in 1993.

As I got to know her, I found her to be a complex person, a unique individual, intelligent *and* smart, creative, hard-working, remarkable in many ways that began to unfold as I learned more about her. Elene was, when we met, in the midst of earning her master's degree in counseling while simultaneously raising her 8-year-old daughter, Danielle, getting sober, starting anew in San Diego, and quickly becoming the matriarch of her family.

Elene's mom had recently been moved into a nursing facility after suffering a terrible stroke, and Elene was thrust into that maternal position with two younger siblings who needed her guidance. She had lost her father several years before—a violent, tragic death she discusses in this book. Elene inspired me to become a better person: If she could improve her lot in life under these circumstances, I could certainly do the same. After floundering around in education for several years, and racking up close to two hundred units that did not add up to a single degree, I finally jumped in to earn my bachelor's.

Our relationship was complicated, and for some time we struggled to know if we would stay together. We had broken up in 1996, and that year I went, without her, to the Whole Being Weekend. I had been thinking a lot about whether or not I would like to have a child, and had come to the conclusion that I did not have a deep need to have one of my own. I distinctly remember telling friends at the retreat that I had come to that realization after a lot of reflection. After driving back down the mountain, life presented me with a different outcome. Elene told me she was pregnant, and she wanted to keep the pregnancy.

Though I had just decided I did *not* want to be a father, I found myself taking the first step in a journey I would not give back for anything: I was about to become the father of Jamie Morgan Mychael Bratton-McNeeley, an event that would open me to a depth of love I never knew existed. This book is, among other things, the story of that little boy, someone who completely changed me, and who had, and continues to have, a powerful impact on so many.

Through everything, the ups and downs in our lives and in our relationship, one thing always held steady. We were both profoundly in love with our son, and we both wanted nothing more than to raise him and

Danielle in the most stable and loving environment possible. As you will read in this book, Jamie lived a pretty wonderful, albeit short, life. He spent time on the road, and in Mexico, right as he was learning to speak, and then followed up on his Spanish learning at The Language Academy in San Diego. He had great friends and family and neighbors around him. Just as things started to really flow and seem somewhat settled for our family, Jamie suddenly died, and our whole world fell apart in an instant.

In *Jamie's Joy: Honoring Grief, Creating Legacy, Celebrating Life,* Elene skillfully describes the unbearable anguish around losing *a* child, and narrates the extreme, deadening hell of losing *ours*. Before Jamie died, Elene had already experienced much painful loss in her life, but none as devastating, as life-threatening, as this loss. When we were able to stand up, we started desperately trying to figure out what to do without Jamie "in his body." Elene describes much of that process here, and I am certain that reading about it will help others living with their own losses. As Elene explains, we are living amongst hordes of people coping with grief in a grief-illiterate society.

"Jamie's Joy" started within a very special little boy, then later became a concept, a website, a loose "organization," and is now a book. All this is meant to remember Jamie, to keep him in the world, to give legacy to someone too young to leave behind his own in a tangible form. Yes, Jamie's Joy exists for that, but even beyond that, Jamie's Joy exists to make the world a better place, to open others to their own grief, to their own compassion, to their own love, peace, joy, and connection.

Jamie's Joy: Honoring Grief, Creating Legacy, Celebrating Life shares the story of one family who lost someone key to its very existence. Elene shows us that choosing to run straight into the pain, fully grieving our losses, can transform who we are in the world. It is indeed possible to emerge from the fire, not unharmed, but certainly into someone who is more empathetic, more sensitive to the pain of others, more able to sit with grief than before, and definitely more capable of living on, even when a loved one has not been afforded that privilege.

As I read through this book, much of the story is one I have lived through, but I also found the narrative refreshingly new in many ways. I laughed and I teared up as I read. I hope this book will inspire you, whether you are moving through your own grief, supporting another through theirs, or are simply becoming a more compassionate, loving person.

May this book help us create a society in which grief is embraced and valued, in which remembering and honoring our most painful losses is welcomed. May this book help those who experience great loss to go beyond survival, and, as Elene has done, to "live life out loud."

With Love,

Mychael McNeeley, Jamie's Dad

Angel by Jan, Mychael's sister

grira Sol

INTRODUCTION

This book is not written in a linear fashion and it is not based on "time" because it is a book about the brokenness and beauty of this adventure we call life. It is also about grieving, healing and the healing process. These things are not a straight line. There are no "ABC" instructions for loss, no "one size fits all" recovery from pain, because the process is purely personal and intimate to the person experiencing it. It is a winding road that no one can follow, as it continually gets washed out by the tears shed along the path behind the person as they keep moving forward, grieving, processing, surviving and, eventually, learning to live beside the loss(es).

This is the account of my journey through the grieving process with its multi-faceted paths. Hopefully you have not suffered the level of loss that my family has, but since no life goes unscathed, my wish is that you find things you can relate to, if loss has been a part of your life—which, it seems, we all must experience at some point. May these points be far and few between, and may you find resilience and hope along your path.

I have developed writing prompts and reflections within the pages of this book for your use, along with resources you may find helpful if grief is part of your life's journey.

Elene Bratton
Jamie's Mom & Co-Founder of Jamie's Joy

Grief is like an Ocean

It is deep

It is wide

It covers most of the surface

It has waves that can be jumped over

It has waves that swallow you up,

Tumbling you about

Making you fight for your life

and spitting you up onto the shore,

when THEY are done with *you*.

Just like the ocean, grief is dark and mysterious

and has many odd creatures in its depths,

things of which we shall never know

The ocean can drown

Grief drowns.

© 2003 Elene Bratton

The family in Merida, 1997. Enjoying the waters of Cancun. Mychael, Jamie's dad, holding Jamie (one-and-a-half years old); Elene, Jamie's mom; Danielle, a.k.a. "Sissy," Jamie's 15-year-old sister; Angela, Jamie's aunt; and Demetri, Jamie's 5-year-old cousin/"brother."

He's Here

Written May 24, 1996 by Uncle "Daven" (how Jamie pronounced "David")

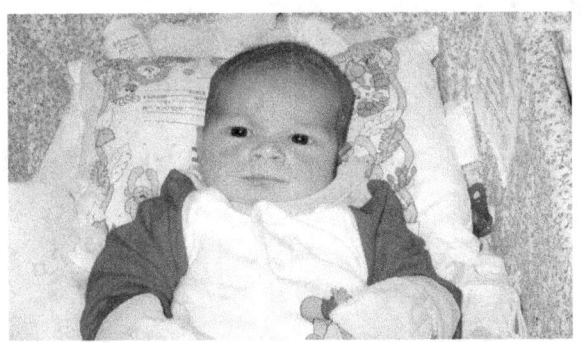

He's here
And what was once inside
Is now out.
It's been two weeks waiting
After nine months anticipating
I can hardly believe
He's here—
Sleeping and pooping and breathing
With his blue remnant
Of an umbilical cord
And uncircumcised penis.
Call up God
And make sure he knows
HE'S HERE! He's here among us—
Line up the trumpets and bugle horns,
Wheel out the blasting parade
And let everyone know
Of this perfect little boy

My nephew, your son, our reason.
You should see him:
Quiet and understanding
He knows something important,
I can tell—
So still and real
So quick to adjust
So much like Buddha
And all the enlightened souls
He's something to behold
So come take a look, hold him
near your heart—
I'm tellin' ya
He's so cool and little and
wrinkled
And best of all
He's here.

© 2002 David McNeeley

CHAPTER ONE

In the Beginning
The Musings of a 5-year-old Buddha

———

When our Jamie Boy was born on May 24, 1996, a level of love opened within us that we never knew existed. Jamie came at a time when our relationship was falling apart. It seemed to us that he had come to help us see how much we could love when we couldn't see that for ourselves. During the pregnancy, it became clear that we were committed to raising our son together in a loving home, embracing being a family. As we committed to this new life, we recommitted to each other. Then it was time to nest. We decorated the baby's room with angels and Winnie the Pooh and we waited for the arrival. (These were the days before the ever-so-popular "gender reveals.")

On the day our very own angel, Jamie, was born, we knew he was an

old soul. He had the deepest eyes, and the smile on his face told you he knew *something*. He seemed very wise. We called him our "Little Buddha."

When Jamie was 17 months old, we rented out our house in the U.S. and made what ended up being a 9-month journey to live in Mexico and travel across the U.S. Jamie's first language was *Spanglish*. He attended Guarderia, a free preschool in our neighborhood of Reparto las Granjas, Mérida, Yucatán.

He was very active at school and around the house. "Shoes bye-bye" was his favorite phrase. He was a sweet boy, always wanting to be close to those he loved. "I wanna *jale* your *pelo*" (I want to hold your hair) he would say at the end of each night as he clutched for the comfort of mommy's hair to soothe himself to sleep. He continued to talk in these Spanglish phrases, coining new words such as *"aguamelon"* and phrases such as *"Mi* want *leche."*

As he grew, he was all boy, but he also seemed to be a deep thinker—possessing abstract thinking, spiritual understanding and self-reflection at a young age. When he was two-and-a-half years old, he spontaneously told me the story of how he picked us as parents. He explained very confidently that he was up in heaven with an angel and that he saw us on the bed. He told the angel that he wanted to be with us and then slid down a long tunnel into my tummy! Luckily, he later (under some pressure) recounted the story on videotape.

Although he had an intellect way beyond his years, Jamie loved jumping off things, making fart jokes, curiously exploring the world and collecting a variety of objects that he stuffed in his pockets. It was a special age and a very special, vivacious life was unfolding.

Jamie attended church with us at Christ Church Unity in San Diego, California, and although he had an early Christian influence, his own teachings were far more universal. Since Jamie was about three years old, if you'd ask him anything about himself such as, "Jamie, why are you so cute (smart, funny, wise, etc.)?" he would always reply, ". . . 'Cuz God made me this way!"

Jamie went to a wonderful preschool called Murphy Canyon run by Steve and Nooshin. His teacher's name was Ms. Cindy. When I would play The Who's song "See Me, Feel Me," Jamie would always sing "Ms. Cindy, feel me . . ." I didn't have the heart to tell him that The Who were not singing, "*Ms. Cindy,*" so he just sang it that way.

In his last year at Murphy Canyon, he broke his arm playing on the big playground turtle with another boy. When our friend Jeanne asked him what happened, Jamie took full responsibility: "I was on the turtle and he was on the turtle and I started to fall and I grabbed onto him and he started to fall, and he fell on my arm and it broke. I shouldn't have done that."

Jamie and I spent time in prayer each morning. At the end of 2000, when President Bill Clinton was leaving office and the Palestinian and Israeli peace plans were falling apart, we had these prayers for peace from a variety of traditions, including those of Jewish and Palestinian faith traditions. I would read the faiths' prayers for peace, that they themselves wrote and supposedly believed in. Jamie and I would ask God to have them just listen to their hearts and follow their own prayers for peace.

We prayed this for several weeks, and one day Jamie simply looked up to me and said, "Mom, they can't hear their hearts. They are too much in war." He really got it! No one can hear their heart when they are "at war" with themselves, their fellows, nature or the world-at-large. How can we follow even our own desire to be our personal best when we are at war inside ourselves and can't listen to our hearts?

We had a "God Can" in our home because, when "we can't, God can!" We would put things in the can that we wanted help with each day during our prayer time, or anytime it was needed. Whenever I asked Jamie what he put in the can his reply was always the same: "fear and *fyster*." I never asked him what "fyster" meant, because it made perfect sense and further validated his reputation as a very old and wise soul.

At night when the sun goes to bed, the moon is awake.
At sunny times, it is the moon's turn to sleep."
—Jamie, 4 years old

Jamie was on a roll. Almost every time we would pray, he would say something very profound. My favorite will always be, "Most people think the world is round, but it's really in the shape of a heart, because it's God's heart."

As a family, you make up all these little phrases and songs as you get to know your kid. There was the "how come" song when he was about two: "My name is Jamie How Come, I like to ask, 'How come?' I like to say, 'Why, why?' My name is Jamie How Come, 'How come? How come? How come?'"

Jamie really got into brushing his teeth (which will come up later in our story in a not-so-good way) and, at this point, he would get his "kid" toothpaste—not the hot (mint) kind—ready on the brush and he would turn around in circles, brushing, so we made up the "I'm a rotating brusher" song. "I'm a little rotating brusher, brushing my front teeth, I am a little rotating brusher, brush, brush, brush." We moved on to front teeth, back teeth, top teeth and even the tongue as the ritual went on for many rotations of our precious little whirling dervish.

He also loved Sponge Bob Square Pants, praying and people, especially family—but if he loved you enough, you were family. He loved skipping rocks and jumping from, well, from just about everywhere. He wanted to

marry his mother and cared deeply about humanity. He also loved a good costume—well, really, he loved just about any costume!

He was the most spiritual and most *human* person I have ever met. Jamie loved all types of music. I remember him coming up

to me beaming with pure joy, "I love Sissy's music (rap and pop), Daddy's music (alternative) and your music." (A bizarre blend of classic rock, new wave 80's and lots of spiritual music, including his favorite, "Kral Antie.")

Jamie's father Mychael and I got married a few days after Jamie's 4th birthday. During the wedding ceremony, after he and his cousin, Alexis, begrudgingly carried the flower basket together down the grassy aisle, Jamie arrived at the altar and shouted, "Mom, your dress looks like a tent." The family and friends that came to witness the happy occasion burst out laughing.

Although he forgot most of his Spanish when we returned stateside, Jamie was reintroduced to his first lingua at The Language Academy, a San Diego magnet school focused on teaching kids a second language by the third grade.

Jamie had quite a sense of humor. He was naturally funny, outgoing and verbal. He made friends easily with all ages and types of people. So many of our friends and neighbors—even with only a single interaction—have great stories of how Jamie touched them in a deep and profound way. We went to a work picnic when Jamie was about 4 years old. We sat with my boss, Richard, and his grown son. His son hit it off with mine and they hung out. He later reported to his father Richard that Jamie and he had a soda together, leading Jamie to profess, "I love my soda, it's so effervescent."

One of my favorite stories is when Jamie went out with our neighbor Patty for a day. She took him to the Cabrillo Monument. Afterward, they were going to go to lunch. She asked, "What would you like to eat for lunch?" Jamie replied, "Well, I don't eat my friends." Jamie was a devout vegetarian, except for the few bologna sandwiches that his aunt snuck him. He respected all of life's creatures, from creepy crawlers to majestic mammals.

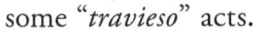

Jamie started The Language Academy in the Fall of 2001, right after "the turtle incident" in which he broke his arm. He still had the cast on when he boarded the bus for his first day of kindergarten. He had many great friends at school, and did well in his studies, but was not without some "*travieso*" acts.

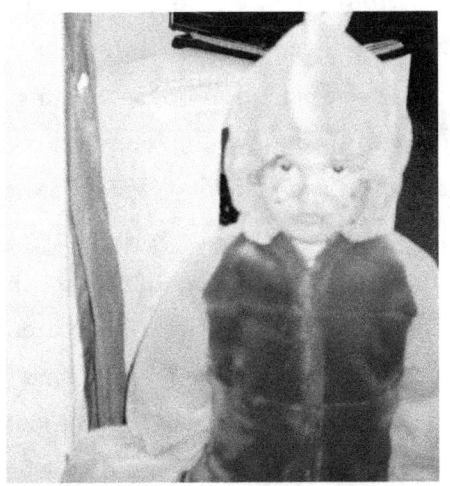

Once, he accidentally spit on the principal from the bus window because his mom told him he had to brush his teeth after lunch. Here's where that dedication to brushing his teeth didn't go so well for him: It so happened to be a short day at school that day, and Jamie felt so compelled to follow directions and brush his teeth that

he decided to do so on the bus. And where is a boy supposed to spit at that point, but out the window? He described it later, "I saw the principal coming, I saw the spit flying, I kept hoping they would miss each other, but they didn't."

There was also the time he was called into the office because he "mooned" one of his classmates. When the principal asked Jamie where he learned that, he truthfully said, "My dad." Mychael then, too, got sent to the principal's office.

Kindergarten was proving to be an overall great time with lots of learning, growing, girl-chasing at recess and finding his first true love (besides mom, of course). Jamie came home one afternoon declaring, "I have a girlfriend." "What's her name?" Mom asked. "I don't know," he innocently answered. Aww, the joys of young love.

We spent weekends hiking and walking our neighborhoods, mornings praying and talking, mealtimes with Jamie running five times around the table between each bite. We called it the "5-Year-Old-Boy Weight Loss Program" and joked about bottling it. We were happy. Life was good.

About six weeks before his 6th birthday he was hanging in the tree in the front yard of our home. Our neighbor and his sometimes-babysitter, Aurora, came upon him there and told him to be careful—"*con quidado.*" They had a long conversation about his plans to marry, what he wanted to be when he grew up (a dentist—or a beekeeper—go figure) and how he planned to celebrate his upcoming 6th birthday, all from the safety of the sturdy limb of the Tipuana Tipu tree that was planted in his honor, by Mychael, when Jamie was six months old. It was growing big and strong, alongside this hilarious, beautiful, healthy, vivacious, smart and spirited young man.

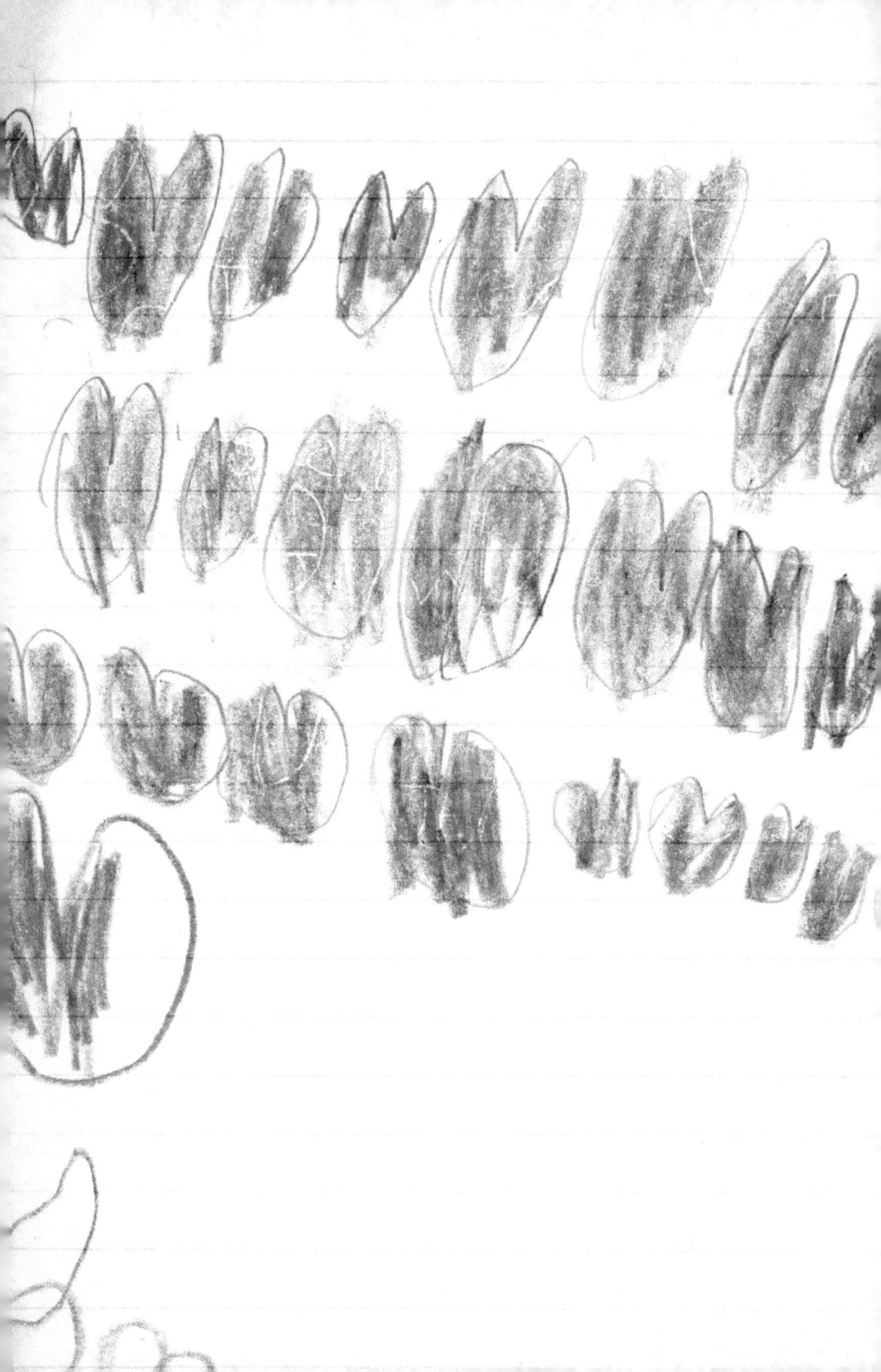

CHAPTER TWO

When Tragedy Strikes

Then just as suddenly as he appeared, he was gone. On April 24, 2002, at approximately 2200, exactly one month shy of his 6th birthday, the life of Jamie Morgan Mychael Bratton-McNeeley was tragically and suddenly over in a car crash.

The day before he was to spend the night with his aunt Angela and cousin Demetri, hanging out at the pool, eating pizza—basically having fun, Jamie got in trouble at kindergarten. We agreed the next morning that he could only go if he did well in school that day. He managed to pull off a "green color" for the day, indicating it was a good day. So Angela picked

When Tragedy Strikes

You loved nakedness
We are naked now
Weeping, and loving you
You are naked now
Free from fear
Fear and Fyster
You let it go
We are all naked now
You loved the heart
Our hearts are here
Broken and open
For all to see
We are naked now
Weeping, and longing for you
You loved nakedness

**For Jamie Morgan from Dad
May 2, 2002**

©2002 Mychael McNeeley

him up after school, put him in the backseat of her small car, and latched his seat belt. Then she drove from San Diego city proper toward the northern part of the county, about forty minutes away, to enjoy family time together.

After exiting the freeway near her home, for some reason that we will never know, Angela lost control of her car. The car veered off to the right side of the road and went up on the pavement. Then it drifted across again, making a left turn and landing in someone's driveway on the other side of a 4-lane throughfare. Just then, a large truck came around a blind curve, hitting the side of the car where Jamie was sitting in the back seat. Angela was less impacted in the opposite side of the vehicle but suffered a severe head trauma (or "TBI") and was taken to one hospital. Jamie was life-flighted to Rady's Children's Hospital.

As I rushed to Children's Hospital on that fatal night, I can remember racing down the freeway, unaware of the seriousness of the situation, foolishly hoping that my sweet son's face was okay. I spent many guilt-filled nights beating myself up later for worrying about his face when, in fact, his body was preparing to leave this plain.

"Why couldn't I stop this?!"

I wondered on those same nights why I couldn't intuitively know that my son was in trouble. We were so connected, I felt I should have sensed something. I should have had a feeling that something was about to go horribly wrong. I should have been able to predict what was coming and not let him take that fateful car ride.

Bottom line: I should have been able to execute the most fundamental job a mother has. I should have been able to protect my son. Even as I read this now, all these years later, the same anguish washes over me: "Why couldn't I stop this?!"

The kindly yet completely ill-equipped-to-handle-this-type-of-loss staff sent us home from the hospital with a box in which to put our keepsakes. I was so angry at the box, and at the culture that stood fiercely incapable of meeting our needs. It was a beautiful and well-intentioned gift, which I quickly stuffed away, without ever inserting anything.

Only years later, while writing this book, did I figure it out: How do you put a little boy's life—along with all your hopes and dreams for a future that will never be—into a (. . . no matter how beautiful or well-intentioned . . .) *fucking box*? That box sits to this day in a cupboard, unused, a vivid reminder of that ill-fated night.

JAMiE's Self Portrait

CHAPTER THREE

Desperate Times Call
for Desperate Measures

F rom the time of the initial news, I knew life would never be the same. I remember not being able to go a moment without thinking of Jamie. Every tree reminded me of his wavy, long hair, every location was a place we had been, every song one we had sung, every food something we had eaten together. Mychael and I couldn't sit still, sleep or think. We had to write everything down. We couldn't cook, shop or pay bills, let alone work. Luckily for us, we both had understanding workplaces that gave us the time off we needed until we could function again— at least well enough to work. Having a compassionate work place allowed us to continue working with these companies. Our doctor put us out on state disability because both of us had jobs where we needed to be able to

think; Mychael climbed trees and I worked in a jail. A wrong move or absent-minded mistake could mean life or death for us or for others we worked with.

Jamie left his body on a Wednesday. The next day, a group of four work friends descended with pure love into our home, bringing practical things we couldn't have thought of, like lots of Kleenex and their presence in what could only be described as the deepest depths of human pain.

Later that week (which I describe as "our descent into Hell"), on Saturday, a group of us from work had been signed up to walk the March of Dimes charity walk. We had all agreed to go—before the tragedy—including my husband, my nine-months-pregnant daughter, and our soon-to-be-6-year-old son. Of course, in the aftermath of what had just befallen us, we didn't even remember the event. But my good friend Mimi Goodman and her family did. They made t-shirts and walked in honor of Jamie and our family. These are the types of friendships that supported us in our initial grief, and this support was enough to keep us here—at least long enough for us to want to still be here.

They made hand-painted t-shirts which read, "I'm marching in Jamie's Shoes" with an image of his boots, which he always left in front when he came home, and continue to remain there to this day.

We were also fortunate to live in a society that has a Family Medical Leave Act (thank you, Bill Clinton) and state disability. We would often think of others around the globe that may be living in war torn areas, where the houses they had lived in with all of their family members had been destroyed by rocket launchers, where everyone else was dead and the survivors were trying to plaster together their home, let alone find a way to heal from unspeakable grief.

"Trying to fill the Grand Canyon with an eyedropper."

We were able, even in those first hours and days, to find compassion for others who may not have had the luxury of staying home to heal. We found gratitude for this opportunity our society afforded us, and as we went about the business of trying to heal, we knew it would take a lifetime. I remember reading a book entitled, *Against the Dying of the Light: A Father's Journey Through Loss*, by Leonard J. Fein wherein he stated that all these things we do in the face of such grief is like "trying to fill the Grand Canyon with an eyedropper,"* but we were making first steps with the time given us.

We catalogued all of our photos, trying to preserve our memories of Jamie. We tucked them away in a fireproof safe, hoping to protect them in ways we couldn't protect our only son. We needed to feel that we could ensure they would be safe from harm—forever. Whatever protection we couldn't give to Jamie during his life, we wanted to ensure for the *memory* of Jamie.

The thought of no more photos, no more memories being made, was heavy on our minds. For years, I refused to have any photos taken. I just couldn't record any events where Jamie wasn't in the picture. Everything felt like "too much." Several friends who innocently tried to offer words of comfort got caught in the middle of our raging grief, being yelled and

---

*(See Chapter 18 "Suggested Reading" for a full list of titles & reviews.)

cussed at for saying things like "he was in a better place" or "God must have needed him" or "isn't it great that he is with Jesus?"

We literally compiled a list of the top 10 most stupid things people said to us. We nailed them to our front door along with a list of how to approach us; this was our Martin Luther reformation moment. We were declaring war on the grief-illiterate world we found ourselves swimming upstream in. We were having to educate our friends on how to support us while at the lowest point of our lives.

As time goes by, I can now see how fortunate I was, and still am, to have had the set of friends I do. They have supported me on my journey all of these years. Not just in the beginning by stopping by and taking care of the basics like shopping, cleaning, cooking, driving, etc., when we were so stuck by grief we couldn't function, but over time by being members of the board for Jamie's Joy, helping organize Jamie's Joy functions, clean-ups at Jamie's Way, riding 50-mile bike-a-thons, selling tickets to family and friends, soliciting donations and much more, but most importantly by remembering Jamie and carrying his legacy to live a life of Love*Joy*Peace*Connection in big and small ways every day. I love and appreciate everyone who has helped make Jamie's Joy a road for us all to walk toward healing together.

A few months after Jamie left his body in 2002, Mychael and I attended an annual spiritual retreat called "Adults of Unity (AOU)" hosted at Unity Village in Missouri. We were both hating ourselves in that moment for having gone in the past and missing any time with Jamie and feeling like he could finally attend the retreat with us now, if only in Spirit. We couldn't be with the group much, so the presenters and participants came to us where we were and we just talked, prayed, grieved, and stayed, through the week.

We were given the opportunity to share the PowerPoint from Jamie's service with his photos. His beautiful, shiny soul touched everyone's heart. It was in these moments I deeply understood the effects of untouched grief. I will never forget all the people who came up to us there—and most times, when I shared my story—who expressed such untouched grief from years of simply not being able to voice what had happened to them. A mother, now in her 60's, who had lost two children to stillbirth 30 years prior, who was never even allowed to see her babies; a sister who had never been able to utter her brother's name again after he passed when they were teens; a woman who had gone to jail because, as she told us, she had lost her husband and simply didn't know how to cope, so she took a note to a bank (to rob them) and waited for the police to arrive. Another woman who came for group support for a loss that happened 30 years prior had previously been running from grief by "escaping" into the casinos.

Sigmund Freud himself had to concede that he needed to reconsider his original theory that one "had to let go, move on and gain closure" over grief when he lost his own child. When Freud lost his daughter Sophie, he wrote a letter to his friend and colleague Ludwig Binswanger in which he explained that, in a way, grief was a way of holding on to love, and, as such, it was better not to let go of it altogether.

Just like so many people, Freud was forced to change his theories about grief. Sophie was 26 when she passed. Of course, this realization by Freud, this revelation through tragic personal experience, came too

late and is far lesser known than his pre-tragedy book on surviving grief that sold millions of copies—and is still in circulation—than his letter written to one colleague wherein his insights into grief were profoundly altered. Unfortunately for me and most of the bereaved, Freud's original theories survived over time and so the conventional wisdom that has persisted is to "just get over it."

More recently, many additional personal letters of Sigmund Freud have been made available online, so hopefully over time his more advanced insights into how grief is best processed can become better understood and accepted by all. In the meantime, thanks to Freud and many others, I have seen firsthand and learned early on in my journey that we live in a "grief illiterate, stuffing feelings and find-a-silver-lining" culture.

Most people don't know what to say or can't talk about their traumatic experiences and losses at all. But somehow I knew, in the midst of such excruciating pain, that I had to find another way. I knew that I had to find a way to *be with the pain, while still seeing the beauty.* To see color, when everything looked bleak and grey.

I had read but never followed the "stages of grief," which psychiatrist Elisabeth Kubler-Ross had written, studying how the *dying* experience grief, not the left-behind, but I've learned there is a lot of overlap of feelings for both those facing their own dying and those experiencing the loss of a loved one. Though I mostly dwelled in the land of sadness, the anger did also appear. One of the most poignant moments was during that first year after Jamie left his body. In my world, that is where the line is drawn.

There is "when Jamie was here" and "after Jamie left his body," and time is divided *right there*.

Anyway, back to the anger: During the 2002 AOU retreat, we were really being nurtured by the group and presenters when we met a man who had also lost his son. That's when the cursing began. Every deeply bereaved person has to pass through this place—a place where you simply scream at the top of your lungs and from the bottom of your heart . . . a place where only the most vile language can express the anguish felt from such egregious loss.

Our moment came in the atrium, outside the chapel, with this man, who had lost his son a few years before us, in the middle of the spiritual retreat. He knew we could never get right with God again unless we had it out right there, right then. So, we screamed and yelled and questioned, cried, hollered and snotted until we were so tired but somehow knew that . . . God wasn't the one. God didn't take our son, God didn't punish us, God didn't hate us. God was wrapping their healing spirit upon us and helping us to heal by finding people that would allow us to embrace all parts of this process, all parts of ourselves. God, Spirit, Higher Power, Life (whatever your preferred term or pronoun) is big enough to withstand

"Tears are salt water from the sea. Because when you go to the ocean the water gets in your eyes, the wind gets in your eyes and blows out all the water. That's all. It's like rain."

—Jamie, 5 years old

our ranting/raving and understanding enough to love us no matter how irreverent we get.

The endless "what ifs" were relentless, choiceless and torture. I constantly kept trying to make what *had* happened *not have* happened by creating a world where, somehow, I intervened and stopped this event in its tracks:

"What if I hadn't let him go with my sister? It was a school night, after all. What parent lets their kid stay the night at someone else's house on a school night?!" "What if he had been in the middle seat?" "What if I had never sold my condo and my sister wouldn't have been living in North County?" "What if I cursed him by naming him Jamie after my female cousin who also died young at the age of 21 in 1983?" "What if I had been a better person . . . then this curse would have passed me by . . ."

"What if, what if, what if . . ."

At some point, I read a book that I recommend above all others for parental grief entitled, *The Worst Loss* by Barbara Rosoff. This book is fundamental for parents who have lost children. It also breaks loss down by type—and for bereaved children, by age—as they are often forgotten mourners. I was so relieved to know that I wasn't going crazy, that I was simply trying to stop the worst thing ever to befall my life. And it was common, normal, even. And it had a name: "un-doing."

Another monumentally important book that helped me to redevelop my relationship with God, whom I call Spirit, was entitled, *When Bad Things Happen to Good People* by Rabbi Harold Kushner. The key idea that helped me update my beliefs was that God, while all-loving and ever present, is not able to control every aspect of human life. For me that was the difference between believing God somehow "took my son" and believing that Spirit could provide comfort to me in my darkest hour. This, more than any other book, sustained my faith while severely altering it.

I can't believe in a God who—however well-suited, for the rest of creation, that taking my son would be—would perpetuate such an act on a parent, let alone the innocent child. Ideas such as "Nothing happens by accident" or "God needed him" that suggest a higher power would purposefully take your child is, to me, cruel at best and evil at its worst.

And while I would never take any of these beliefs away from people for whom they are a healing balm, *they were shards of glass stabbing me in the heart again and again.* My God is not cruel or evil. My God does not take the people you love. Alas, dying is assured from conception: We don't know when and we don't know how. What is so amazing to me is that, although we are aware that this fate will come to us and to those we give our hearts to—especially our children, we continue to give our hearts freely, again and again, knowing they can be broken, over and over. This is what it means to be human. *This is the true miracle of life.*

That is the Spirit I know, the Spirit I believe in, the Spirit that sustains me . . . loving, comforting, nurturing, supportive—and resilient.

While my concept of God is so much more relatable for me now versus being set on strict beliefs, it is ever-evolving. Like any relationship, it's not perfect, it doesn't explain everything, and it certainly doesn't take all the pain away, but it does allow me to have faith.

That first year after Jamie left his body, Mychael and I craved to stay connected to Jamie and asked to hear all of the stories about Jamie that friends and family had to tell, and these stories were written down. We also wrote down everything we could remember about our beloved son, including his last five days, which is so-titled and included in the "stories" chapter of this book (Chapter 13). We made scrapbooks, and we eventually created a website developed to honor Jamie (www.jamiesjoy.org).

Desperately seeking answers, we went to psychic readers, watched John Edward's psychic/medium show religiously, read books profusely, took classes on meditation and connections to the spirit world. We combed the obituaries looking for children who had passed away and called or paid visits to funerals of grieving families—families we didn't even know, but knowing the depth of pain they were experiencing, making what I later called "the descent into hell," we were compelled to share the little resources we had with them. Looking back, I can see we were crazed, crazed with grief. We wanted—no, needed—to talk about our shared experience, offer mutual support and comfort one another.

But alas, it was just as Leonard Fein had described in his book—it can feel like trying to fill the Grand Canyon with an eyedropper. Or as Jamie's 5-year-old friend Tyler put it upon hearing the news, as she looked frantically from face to face at the caregivers who were saying things that were supposed to make everything better: "Nothing helps."

But eventually it all did, at least a little. Thich Nhat Hanh states it this way: "Don't ignore your suffering but don't forget to enjoy the wonders of life . . ."

Jamie's room remained untouched for many years, and, in fact, is still "his room": We converted it into an office for Jamie's Joy. Winnie and the angel gang are in one corner, as awards and Jamie's Joy accolades take up space where diplomas and STEM awards should have hung. It is a mix of what was, what will never be, and what is. The "grands" (my grandchildren) toss the stuffed animals about now, and jump into the bean bag chair, and guests spend the occasional night there. All a constant reminder of Love*Joy*Peace*Connection.

COUNTY OF SAN DIEGO
DISTRICT ATTORNEY

Certificate of Recognition

presented to

ELENE BRATTON

The San Diego County District Attorn...
proud to honor your civic engagement a...
contributions to the Jamie's Joy Mem...
on this Eighth Day of June, 2013 and he...
the 5th Annual Make a Joyful Noise Fam...
which celebrates the legacy...
Jamie Morgan Mychael Bratton-...
through love, joy, peace, and conn...
empowers youth in the San Diego c...

June 8, 2013

Bonnie M...

Jamie
Morgan
Mychael
Bratton-
McNeeley

Forever in Our Hearts
www.jamiesjoy.org

Jamie's Way

On March 23, City Council unanimously approved changing Marlborough St. to honor our littlest Parkster, Jamie Bratton-McNeeley, who most of you know died tragically in a car accident on April 24, 2002.

Thank you to Albert Franco who donated his time to do the required architectural drawings of the site for the City review. The family is paying for all related costs of the name change and Albert saved them a lot of money with his generous donation. Call Linda Pennington for information at 563-4014.

...ie's Way Dedication

Families, friends, City officials, Com-... ...tives and our very own District 3 Dep-... ...kins gathered to dedicate Jamie's Way. ...the street, leading up to the entry way ...on which has become a place of beauty ...me of three artistic benches has been ...of the trail that winds down the canyon ...se benches have been placed on Poplar ...affords the opportunity to stop a while ...'s bench. Gazing out at the canyon and ...culously manicured landscape it is easy ...all it takes to have a positive influence ...y are positive choices. Jamie had many ...to give his friends, and it is our fortune

to have a place where we can go to reflect not only on his words, but of our own as well.

"people can't hear their hearts when they are too much in war."

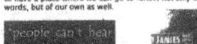
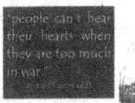

Azalea Park Neighborhood Association
2596 Violet Street, San Diego, CA 92105
Email: info@AzaleaPark.org
Website: www.AzaleaPark.org

The City of San Diego
Proclamation
Jamie's Joy
August 27, 2016

Presented By
The Office Of
Councilmember
Marti Emerald

WHEREAS, Jamie Morgan Mychael Bratton-McNeeley was born May 24, 1996 and was killed in a car crash one month shy of his sixth birthday on April 24, 2002; AND

WHEREAS, in 2003, a committee of family and friends formed to continue Jamie's legacy by creating Jamie's Joy Memorial Fund through the San Die... Foundation; AND

WHEREAS, Jamie's Joy was created in memory of a boy whose physi... presence was cut short but whose spiritual presence continues strongly... everything this organization does; AND

WHEREAS, Jamie's Joy is an organization dedicated to p... light, and legacy of a five year old boy who touched many li... continues to touch our hearts with his spirit of peace, love, ... AND

WHEREAS, the committee gives an annual donation at... birthday to a non-profit organization through the San D... Jamie's name; AND

WHEREAS, this year Jamie's Joy donated their funds to... a program which is dedicated to helping homeless transit... street, heal, and be a productive part of society; NOW, TH...

BE IT PROCLAIMED, that I, City Councilmember M... proclaim August 27, 2016 to be "Jamie's Joy Day" o... residents of District 9.

IN WITNESS WHEREOF, I HAVE HEREUNTO SET...
AND HAVE CAUSED THE SEAL TO BE AFFIXED...

MARTI EMERALD
COUNCILMEMBER, NINTH DI...
August 27, 2016

DATE

COUNCILMEMBER TODD GLORIA
Special Commendation
Presented to

Jamie's Joy

In honor of the life of
Jamie Morgan Mychael Bratton-McNeeley

~

He continues to enrich our
lives through supporting
...ganizations
...oy, love,
...d peace.

May 23, 2009

★ KENSINGTON ★ NORMAL HEIGHTS
UNIVERSITY HEIGHTS

County of San Diego
California
PROCLAMATION
Presented By Supervisor Ron Roberts

HONORING JAMIE'S JOY

WHEREAS, in 2002 the unthinkable happened to Mychael McNeeley and Elena Bratton when Jamie Morgan Mychael Bratton-McNeeley, the couple's 5-year old son, was killed in a car accident; and

WHEREAS, after losing their healthy little boy, Mychael and Elena chose to channel their grief and created Jamie's Joy Memorial Fund in 2003, with the mission to honor the life of Jamie by enriching the lives of all living beings through supporting activities and organizations that promote joy, love, connection and peace; and

WHEREAS, each year, for the last five years, Mychael and Elena have hosted the Make a Joyful Noise fundraiser so that they may continue in their mission and honor Jamie's life; and

WHEREAS, this year marks the 4th annual Make a Joyful Noise fundraiser with all the proceeds going to their mentorship programs for at-risk teens, The District Attorney's Youth Advisory Board and The Somali-Bantu Association; and

WHEREAS, throughout the year, additional grants are given to Save a Child Foundation, as well as community programs that help break the barriers of such as Rady's Children's Hospital HOPE program, The Jamie Drake Foundation and The Compassionate Friends; and

WHEREAS, the County of San Diego is committed to recognizing and honoring those organizations that are dedicated to the best ideals of public service, and Jamie's Joy is one such worthy organization; NOW THEREFORE,

BE IT PROCLAIMED, by Chairman Greg Cox and all members of the San Diego County Board of Supervisors on this 23rd day of May 2013, that they commend JAMIE'S JOY AND THE McNEELEY AND BRATTON FAMILIES for their outstanding commitment, leadership and service to area residents, and do hereby declare this day to be "JAMIE'S JOY DAY" throughout San Diego County.

Feliz

Cumple-
años
te quiero
mucho
Jamie

CHAPTER FOUR

Finding the Soft Landings
& Stepping Stones

When you come to the edge of all you know, you must believe in one of two things: There will be earth upon which to stand or you will be given wings. —O.R. MELLING

In our minds, we want to believe we can count on certain people in our lives to be there when we need them. A parent, a spouse, a sibling, a friend. That, in their role, they should be there for us. It doesn't seem to matter whether or not they were ever able to do that in the past, we need them again *today*—and this will be the day they can do it. Then, we get mad at them, or ourselves, frustrated and surprised that we're not getting our needs met, focusing on having the person who is "supposed to" do it, do it. And a lot of people, including myself, have gotten stuck here, allowing the fact that this didn't happen ruin our lives.

The line of reasoning may go, "My (parent, spouse, sibling, friend) wasn't there for me. I was abandoned in my hour of need." From there it continues, "If they don't care, then no one cares," and from there, "I am not worth caring about." We get mad, feel hurt, then shut down and can't look around to see "from whence our help may come." We give up and say we "don't need anything from anyone!" Not so fast. What if we were able to let go of the notion that the caring, love and support we need—and have needed from the time of our birth—has to come from a specific someone in a certain role in our life, especially if it has never previously been provided by the person it was "supposed" to have been provided by due to their role as parent, spouse, sibling or friend?

Dad: "Jamie, what's the difference between the brain and the mind?" Jamie: "Well, we all have a little bad in us and a little good. The brain is a little bad and the mind is a little good."

Can we be open to the possibility that love and support has actually *been provided* every time we've been in need? Maybe not by the person it's "supposed" to come from, but that it did come. What IF, and here is where we often get stuck, what IF we are open and able to receive and recognize that someone, or perhaps even *something*, is already there to catch us when we fall or hold us through the night?

I had my epiphany sometime after my son Jamie suddenly and unexpectedly left his body on April 24, 2002 in that tragic motor vehicle crash. I immediately sought comfort from the community of friends that I had.

I called my pastor and best friend who met us at the hospital. As word went out, many people descended upon our home to help bring us comfort or meet our practical and emotional needs.

During that initial period, even in the intense grief that was upon us, we noticed that some people were better at providing the practical needs—they answered phones, cooked food, went to the store and swept the floor. Others could sit with us in a space of grief so raw and intense it was blood curdling. We would howl, scream, cuss, cry, and blow our noses into mounds of tissue that formed endless piles all over the floor. The emotion was so raw and so extreme that I am not sure how we survived those first few months I termed "our descent into hell." And there were those who hung in with us, cried with us, sat silent as we rambled and held us tight as we tried to breathe. Karl Anthony was inspired to write two songs: "Jamie's Joy" and "Hold On to Each Other" that talk about who Jamie is and that kind of support.*

As the crowds thinned over time, some folks continued to check on us, stop by for a visit, call to say hello, send cards and keep the floor swept. I also noticed that key people who I thought were good friends had either never shown up or had now disappeared. I remember thinking at the time, when I could think, that there were some folks coming around who I hadn't seen in years, acquaintances who turned into friends. I felt closer to these people more now than at any time in my life, while the others who had been "good friends" were simply . . . gone.

My friends in my recovery fellowship and my sponsor of 14 years, dear friends I had lived life with, my therapist community, and many in my spiritual community, were among some of the folks that could not bear

---

*See Chapter 17 for lyrics to "Hold On to Each Other."

the pain of our pain. People who I thought "should" or would be there for me through it all, through thick and thin, were not.

Questions of doubt kept circling in my mind: "If you can't count on your friends in your time of greatest need, then what are friends really for?" "If a therapist can't handle this, who can?" "If AA can't get me through this type of challenge, how can I get through it?" "If this is too painful for *them*, what about *me*? How will I survive the loss of my son?!" These and many more questions of faith in human nature and the nature of relationships, support and connection swirled within me.

I also questioned my faith and the philosophies that had guided me and made sense for many years which had gotten me through many previous painful experiences in my life—the idea that God was omnipotent, omnipresent, omniscient and everything was in divine order, or "just as it should be."

And I instantly knew that this tragedy (which is entirely too small a word to ever describe what happened) would never fit neatly into that belief. How could hopelessly "out of order" ever BE "in order," let alone be "for the good," even over time? As fictional character Ana ben Matthias said in "The Book of Longings" by Sue Monk Kidd: "I could no longer believe in the God of punishments and rescues." And, I'll add to that, ". . . or the God of miracles for some and the purposeful taking of others." No, NO, I definitely needed something else to understand this one.

Through reading and processing endlessly, I nurtured a new philosophy and coined a phrase that helped me cope with my loss and still believe in a higher power: "God is not an Entity that controls, but a Spirit that Connects." It reflects the idea that there is value in connection, that we are connected to a higher presence, but that there is no God that controls who lives and dies, and therefore did not "take my son" for some reason that is supposed to be "good" for me, when I will always believe that to be a cruel and horrible act of fate: It did happen for a reason—a physical reason. Because a big truck hit a little car.

It was not an act of God that determined my son needed to die that day "for some reason" that I am just supposed to accept or be okay with, and even embrace, because "God is in control" and not only decides who lives and dies but intervenes to prevent death for some while allowing others to die in all types of horrendous ways. Not to mention all other kinds of "favors" given or withheld. This doesn't sound like a God—this sounds more like a mob boss.

> *"God is not an Entity that controls,*
> *but a Spirit that Connects."*

I developed an intense craving for connection, for closeness to my husband, and I looked for ways to talk to other parents who suffered the same loss. Surely someone must be able to understand the depth of feeling I was having.

These feelings can only be truly understood by others who have suffered a profound loss, because they literally aren't available unless you've had this deep of a grief. I liken it to being thrown out of an airplane (except not into bright clear skies, but into a dark tunnel), freefalling with no parachute through all these intense, dark, uncomfortable emotions, which are recognizable but have never been felt as intensely, and the unbearable pain—not knowing when or if you are ever going to land.

To this need, we combed websites, talked to complete strangers who we learned had lost children, and read many, many books that brought some comprehension of the magnitude of our journey. We watched films about loss. We took a crash course on what grief would do to us. We found a local support group run by a psychologist, Dr. Ken Druck, who had also lost a child (in a car crash). He founded The Jenna Druck Foundation, which served the community for 11 years, as well as a worldwide organization called, The Compassionate Friends (TCF), which I still attend. We went to workshops, conferences, yoga practices, family grief camps, individual and family therapy and support groups all focused on how to survive the horrific loss of our 5-year-old son, Jamie.

This included EMDR, which I really did find useful. EMDR stands for "Eye Movement Desensitization and Reprocessing" which is an evidence-based therapy tool used for trauma. Even though I never actually saw the accident scene—what I had seen was Jamie's body in the hospital—the mind is a very creative "creature": In my mind, I kept visualizing Jamie in the car—seeing the truck coming and being terrified—and then remembering the sight of his body in the hospital. During EMDR sessions, I was able to process how I kept seeing the accident and Jamie's fearful expression. EMDR helped me to move past all of those visions, to move past my actual sight of him at the hospital, and, instead, to finally just see him at peace. I highly recommend EMDR to work through past or "fresh" trauma.

> *". . . in the beginning of great loss looms an inevitable torture chamber (of) guilt . . ."*

Dr. Druck knew that, in the beginning of great loss, looms an inevitable "torture chamber" where your guilt, "what ifs," angry words, hurts and anguish would haunt you—and it is choiceless. As a bereaved parent, you will go there repeatedly. Just like in the "Autobiography in Five Short

Chapters" by Portia Nelson, you are bound to fall in the same hole over and over again.

In time, though, you can choose to either stay in the torture chamber or make the choice toward life, toward healing, toward love, toward honoring your child by deciding to step away from torturing yourself and instead seeing yourself as surviving this and making the most of the life you do have, and honoring your child *with* that life.

Eventually, over many months (and years), we were able to resume some semblance of a normal life. The support of my husband, family, close friends and the group support we found in the bereaved parent community sufficed for quite some time. I was finally getting my bearings on the long road of healing.

As for Jamie's dad and I, we did it together as husband and wife, as Jamie's parents, as two people on the same path, until we didn't. I guess every journey has its twists and turns, its bumpy roads and dead ends. After two-and-a-half years of healing together, my partner/husband of fifteen years decided he needed to go his own separate way.

Just the thought of another loss was too much for me to bear. At first, I simply curled up and waited for the pain of life to finish me off. It felt as if life was equivalent to a domestic violence relationship and it was time for me to finally leave it. My reasoning went like this:

"If this were a domestic violence relationship, everyone would encourage me, support me, even plead with me, to leave. But because it is life that keeps beating me down, I'm just supposed to take it. And not only that, I am also supposed to somehow make something *better, okay, good, honorable* or *decent* from it. SCREW THAT! I just want it to end."

I was completely broken, beyond despair and seriously suicidal. My friend and Jamie's godmother, Julie, put herself on personal suicide watch to make sure I made it through those darkest hours.

Several months after Mychael's departure, I noticed I was still here. But I really didn't know where to turn to heal from the overwhelming stress I was feeling. I just realized I was alive, I was surviving. The thought of trusting my body to know how to, and be capable of, handling this new crisis while continuing to grieve the loss of Jamie (along with all of life), somehow came to mind. I say "somehow," but I really need to give credit to Dr. Ken Druck for teaching me that grief was an organic process that our bodies have handled for tens of thousands of years of evolution. And this was just another loss. If I simply listened, my body had the answers, and not only that, my body had the power to help me heal. This philosophy continues to sustain me to this day.

Soon after that, I met a new friend at work, she was a runner. I was never "a runner" and hadn't run in years, but at that point I was willing. Running became my new best friend (as you'll see in the next chapter). The next year, while hiking with two good friends, Jeff and Lorenzo, one of them (Jeff, I think) suggested we ride the Baja Fun Bike Ride to honor Jamie. It coincided with the anniversary of his passing. Wow. That became the first year I was able to face that day on the calendar with more than just dread on my heart.

As I started trusting my body, I decided that my mind, Spirit and emotions had just as much wisdom. That, collectively, these make up my intuition, my inner guide or my "still, small voice." I slowly started to trust this inner guide—that it knew where to find avenues for my healing in each moment. In each decision. In each circumstance. I began to affirm that my Spirit also had the ability to know how to and be capable of taking care of me in each moment. I remembered the words of Ken Druck, "Surviving (grief) is the first way to honor your child."*

Dr. Druck also explained that our bodies have learned through tens of thousands of years of evolution how to survive and live beside not only the loss of a child, but all losses. The key lies in not halting the process with addictive or avoidant activity while, at the same time, allowing for bouts of discomfort, numbness and distraction as they come.

We must allow ourselves to *be with* our uncomfortable feelings. It's okay to allow ourselves the reprieve of being numb when it comes. It is a momentary gift and doesn't diminish our love or loss. We also need to allow ourselves to be temporarily distracted. (The loss will come back into focus again soon enough.) "Distraction," as opposed to avoidance, is temporary and allows room or healing to happen and for laughter to return.

With my house now completely empty, I felt very alone and isolated, so I decided to take in roommates. I asked my family back home. My sister and nephew came to live with me again before moving out for the final time a few years later. I have been fortunate (most of the time) to have a series of really fine folks to share my home with me, including my good friend, Julie, who has been by my side for much of this journey. Each one has brought a sense of community and added their touch to my home. I continue to pray that my home always be a place of warmth and welcome, beauty and order, love and community.

I re-entered the realm of romance and have dated and loved some incredible men over the past few years, healing much of the complete sense of failure and shame I was left with after the ending of my marriage.

---

*See end chapters for numerous coping/grieving strategies and healing tips.

My neighbors, Tom and Larry, have sweetly taken on the role of paternal approval for the men in my life.

I had become so afraid of new people. People who didn't know Jamie or my story. I didn't want to have to explain myself and wasn't comfortable around people who didn't know what I was going through, and continued to experience over time in my healing journey, as well as my dedication to an ongoing relationship with my son. Not everyone can understand all of that. But, in time, I opened myself to new friendships and have met some really incredible people, mostly women friends—friends who are willing to take the time to get to know Jamie and love Jamie even though they never met him in life. (As Jamie used to say, "Is that just on TV or is that in life?") They have connected with Jamie's Joy and have felt the love of his essence. They have embodied and helped spread Jamie's message of Love*Joy*Peace*Connection. And they have given their time to volunteer countless hours at fundraisers and service projects.

Some of my dear friends have also left their bodies since I began to write this book. I am thinking of Erica and Ronda. I know Jamie recognized them and greeted them with a big smile and a hug. For many years, I didn't have room to miss anyone except my son. Now my heart is big enough again to miss others bedsides Jamie. I have a collection of friends and family that have since left their bodies whom I miss deeply, none as deeply as him, of course, but well-missed all the same. Love and grief are linked and have a big tent, as big as your heart, and it will make room to continue to love and attempt to connect with those who have moved on, until we are all together on the same plane. All those who have touched me deeply remain my friends, much as I have a relationship with God, who I can't see. I choose to have continued relationships with those, like Jamie, who no longer live in a body, but remain ever-present in spirit.

In processing all of these experiences, thoughts and feelings from
years of healing from heart-
wrenching grief, I noticed something. Even though it is not always
from the source from which I wanted
it to come, support did show up. It

showed up in connection to living beings, in ideas, in positive activities, in
new philosophies being discovered or formed in my thinking. It showed
up in something I read, or a connection I made, in a song I discovered,
or a workshop I attended. It showed up in walks in nature and times of
meditation. In small, quiet ways and huge gestures. It comes when I am
open and looking for it and sometimes despite my shutting down. It comes
when I trust. I now realize and recognize that there are those beings, philosophies and activities that provide the next steppingstone on the path of
my healing journey.

When I think I am alone, or walking to the edge, I just have to reach
out, to take the next step and I will find that soft landing that will aide
in my healing and take me, once again, to the next step in learning to
live again.

Mi mamá me
canta angelito.

CHAPTER FIVE

How Running Saved My Life

———

You've heard the saying, **"Run for your life,"** right? Well, for me, when events disrupted my life deeply, I did. I literally *ran* because my life depended on it. As I mentioned in the last chapter, there were several steppingstones involved in my journey to heal, and one of those came to me via a new friend I made at work named Gina.

Gina was a runner. In fact, she was a tri-athlete. To tell the truth, I really just wanted someone to talk to, but her condition was that we had to do our talking on the trail, running. I hadn't run in years but I was willing to go, just to have an ear to bend. She was so generous to listen to me crying and talking through the first run we did together. As it turned out (which it does if you've lived any length at all), she, too, had survived heartache. She had, in fact, turned to running for solace.

She really helped me process my grief, but Gina's real goal of getting me back up on my feet (literally) was also set in motion! At first, I could barely run a few miles. Although we paced well together at a 10-minute mile ("I'm a slow runner" she would generously tell me), at some point she would speed off to do a 6-mile run, leaving me in her dust. She continued to encourage me and nurture me toward running. And it worked. I caught the "running bug"—or perhaps it was the so-called runner's high—whatever it was, I was hooked!

And running worked. I always felt better after a run. Although I had good and bad days (of depression), I noticed that as I ran, a lot of "fear and fyster" and hurt dropped away. It was as if my Spirit could talk to me (or maybe I could finally listen) when my head cleared during the runs. I don't know if it was actually a "runner's high," but it sure was good therapy. Ideas of forgiveness, letting go, and times of peace would enter my being.

As I ran, I felt free.

"Did you know the wind is just God's air?"
—Jamie, 4 years old

Gina talked me into signing up for a 5k run called the Carlsbad 5000. On the way to the start line, I asked her what a good time would be for a 5k race. "8-minute mile would be good," she replied. I finished the race with a 7:52-minute-mile pace, receiving an extra medal for being one of the first 75 runners to finish.

After that, I was totally hooked. I decided that 2½ months would be time enough to gear up for my first marathon. I signed myself up for the Rock 'n' Roll Marathon in San Diego. I hadn't run past 6 miles yet, but I started running distances to get up to 21 miles before the race. My 21-mile run on Mother's Day of 2006 was to Sea World, to meet my family (who thought I was nuts). It was on that day that I wrote the poem that accompanies this story.

At that time in my training, I didn't even have a Walkman, iPod or MP3 player. *Nada!* I just had the road and my thoughts. But they were healing and powerful thoughts. I was processing all that had happened to me. When I later learned and trained in EMDR therapy, turns out it was developed by a runner and psychotherapist who discovered that the process of running (through Central Park in New York) helped to desensitize trauma memories. What do you know, real life and science meet again! All I know for sure is that running worked and I was addicted. Running became my passion. I ran to reduce stress, I ran to heal, I ran to live.

On race day, I had several friends and family members cheering me on, and Jamie's cousin (my nephew), Demetri, ran the last few miles with me. I had painted my son's website and "26.2" for Jamie on my legs. I felt like I was doing this for him, but more than that, I was doing it to prove to myself that I could live. As the miles went on, I met so many beautiful folks running alongside me—barefoot runners, team runners, other first-time runners and a runner who had been running marathons almost every day for the past month.

Since that first 5k, I've run three marathons, multiple half marathons, dozens of 5- and 10k's, one biathlon (run and swim), a mini-tri and have

ridden my bike up to 66 miles. I've run in Europe, along the Seawall in Cuba, around the island of Zanzibar in Africa, around the Himalayas in Rishikesh and in many other places around the globe, as well as right in my own backyard. Even after having back surgery at the end of 2007, I got back on the road.

I may still dream of someday catching up to my friend Gina in a full triathlon or a 100-mile marathon, but my favorite run will always be barefoot on the beach with a nice dip in the ocean afterwards. Those are my "Forrest Gump" runs, when I feel I can go forever. And while this may be beyond my reach as the aging process takes hold, I continue the journey with my body leading the way. I simply walk and hike more and run less. I've hiked the Camino in Spain, Machu Picchu in Peru, Kilimanjaro in Tanzania, Torres de Paine in Chile and most recently the Great Wall in China.

I can't say that running has totally cured me from feeling the pain of all that has passed, but it literally and figuratively saved my life during a crucial moment when I needed it. I just don't think I would have made it through that painful period of time without the

powerful tool that running has been for me. I also believe that physical movement, in some form, has been there for many others coping with grief. It is so amazing that, built right into our own bodies, is everything we need to heal. We just have to, literally, chase it down—or follow the cues Spirit gives us, whatever the case may be.

I Run

Breakfast in bed, a rose on the tray served by a beautiful sister so full of love and loyalty.

A mother full of rage toward her son, "You nigga, payback is a mother fucker!" The boy cringes in shame on the city bus bench.

I run to absorb it all, the shock of the hard cement is felt in my bones.

Beautiful African violets left on my doorstep by persons who no longer exist, bringing sweet memories of times when I thought we were inseparable.

Mother possum dead on the side of the road, her litter of pups prematurely expelled onto the asphalt.

The delighted smile of a little boy seeing the black and white form of "Free Willy."

I run to integrate all I have experienced, the shock, hurt, beauty, resting on my heart.

A dad hits his son's head: "You're done!" he says, the small boy looking so internally injured, "Why did you hit me, Dad?"

A greeting from friends long past brings memories of fondness, missing, love—and longing again for former closeness.

The delightful taste of cookies and chocolate bring ecstasy to our mouths.

The smile from a stranger brings a feeling of sexiness to my body.

I run to dissipate into the air, to soften the shock of sensitivity to this
world and all its cruelty and wonder.

Don't worry, little possum, there will be more $400,000 condos built in the
flood plains, the land you once called home.

I run to contemplate that I am aware of it all. That I feel joy and pain in ways
that are profound, that the degree I suffer is to the degree I feel joy.

So, I keep running. I run the distance.

I run 26.2 (for Jamie).

I run

I run

I run.

© Elene Bratton, 5/14/06

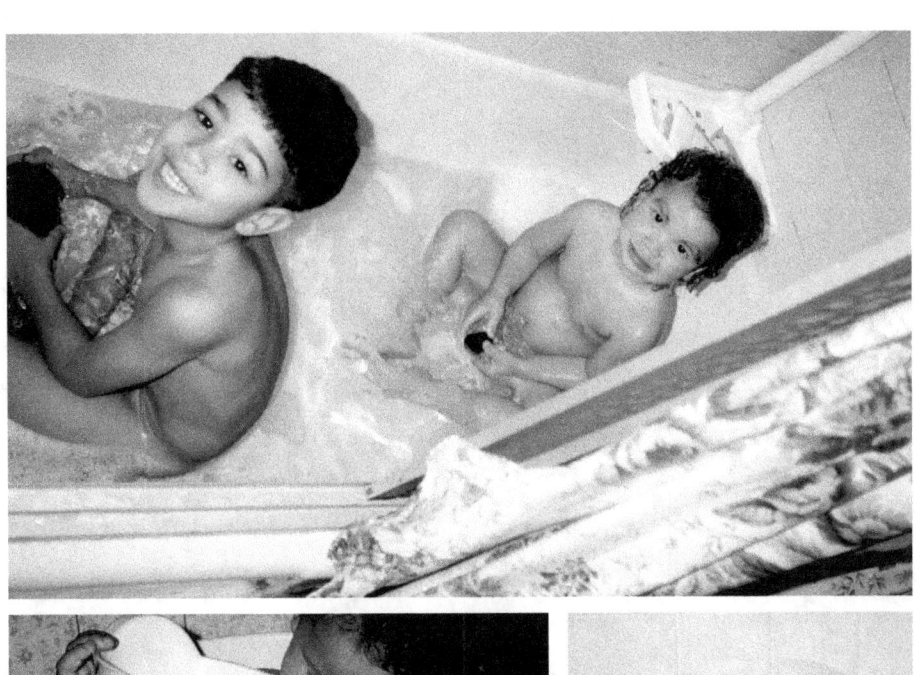

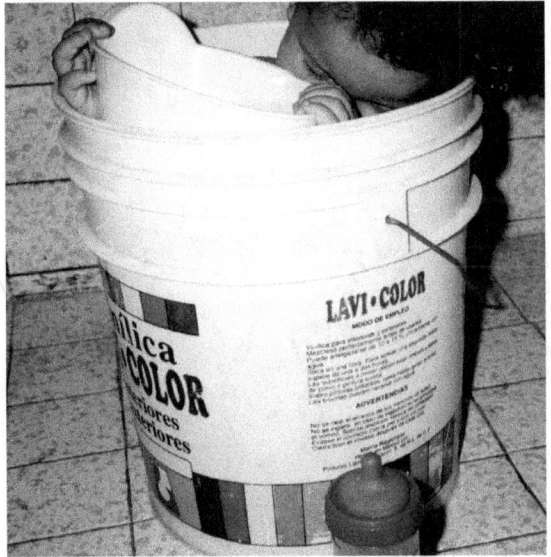

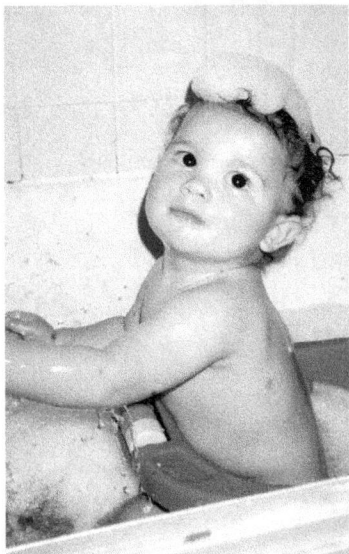

"I am as clean as a pig!"

—Jamie

Para
Papá

CHAPTER SIX

Dimes & Butterflies

W hen we first started going to support groups for bereaved parents, people would say, "Look for pennies from heaven, they are signs from our children." Mychael and I talked about this idea and scoffed it off. "Pennies are everywhere, how can that be a sign?" We thought that, perhaps if we found a *dime* it would be more significant, as they aren't as "throw away" as pennies. Suffice it to say, I have subsequently found dimes in the strangest of places— or at times of the most need. I once found a dime on top of a post in the middle of a hiking trail, way out in the middle of nowhere, letting me know that Jamie was with me on the trail. I often find dimes when I am stressed, upset or hurt. I know that is Jamie telling me, "It's going to be alright, Mom."

Others see butterflies or humming birds buzzing around as signs coming from their loved ones. I do, too. One Easter there was one particular butterfly hovering around my grands (what I affectionately call my grandchildren) as they ran looking for eggs at the church. In addition to dimes and butterflies, I started noticing heart-shaped things, mostly rocks, but also heart-shaped potato chips, fried vegetables, leaves—even heart-shaped animal dung! I recently noticed, yet again, a heart-shaped chip on the sidewalk at work, and during a hike in Yosemite found a heart-shaped wild mushroom patch. It is so random the number of odd things that can be heart-shaped. During that same seven-day Yosemite backpacking trip, I found a piece of shale rock with a "J" written on it. It has to be a sign, right?

We had created several tributes to our son in the front yard and, at some point, Mychael wanted to move the artifacts to a more private location. One of them was a cross we had made from two sticks that Jamie used to play with in the yard. This cross had his photo attached, and Mychael placed the cross in the backyard next to a dead avocado stump. This avocado stump had been that way since we moved into the home some 12 years earlier. About six months later, on a routine surveying of the yard, I saw that the same, "dead" tree had new growth on the wood! I couldn't believe it, and while it still hasn't given any

fruit, with a little TLC it has turned into a leafy avocado bush.

Often people turn to psychics at a time of profound loss. That need to connect with lost loved ones—to know they are all right, that they are still there—is extremely compelling. I spoke of watching endless shows featuring John Edwards, Sylvia Browne and others. We also went to see psychics. I did feel that they connected us with Jamie. The information was too personal or mysterious for them to randomly know it. I also mentioned how skeptical we were about "signs" that were very common like "pennies from heaven," so we were very guarded and didn't give much away.

Having said I believe, I still had trouble with the experience for several reasons. It was never enough. It always left me so emotionally drained, and I still had the same sadness and longing. It didn't seem to relieve my grief.

Some of them made unrealistic promises. That, too, left me disappointed and hurt. Some, I felt, had an agenda about what I was supposed to do to "let go" or "not hold my son back" which left me feeling guilty and judged, with doubt about my process. I don't think grieving people need that, as we are in a very vulnerable emotional state and it's difficult to ward off and unhelpful to hear when you have no emotional skin. After I hadn't been to a psychic in years, I tried again and got #3—feeling guilty and judged. So, while I do feel they reached Jamie, I also feel they don't always act as a pure vessel but, rather, they relate the experience of "Jamie" through their own "BS" (belief systems) and may intentionally or unintentionally say unhelpful things.

I think that, while it might not be a "reading," we can each talk directly to our loved ones. It's a relationship. It has to be nurtured and tended to.

I have known since the beginning of my journey that I would not allow myself or another to dismiss my relationship with my son just because he no longer has a physical form. That is why I say "he left his body." He still exists, just not in his human body. And I have to admit, it is much harder, because I was really accustomed to that form.

As a human animal, I think it is hard to believe things are *real* unless we can touch, taste, smell, see and hear them. But we can, and must, try to maintain some form of bond; maybe not the preferred medium (no pun intended), but we can form a bond with the loved ones we grieve over.

I believe the hearts follow me everywhere because Jamie loved hearts and drew them constantly. Often the hearts I find are uniquely shaped like the hearts Jamie drew, which also makes them feel more real, as if he is here, which I want deeply to believe, even though I still have a tinge of doubt. I think this is another of the complex ways grief exists—and co-exists with hope. We believe our "lost" loved ones are with us while simultaneously wondering, "Is this really true?" knowing that, either way, it's just not the same. I recently adopted a cat with a heart shaped nose.

This is a perfect illustration of my "both/and" insight to come from this experience: We as humans are capable of holding both sorrow and joy; complete devastation and hope, simultaneously. It seems to be a part of our complex capacity as humans. "Both/And" is so important in the world of profound loss because you will experience so much grey area in forming a new identity through loss. I *both* have two children . . . *and* one child. I am *both* always grieving *and* healing. I am *both*  bearing the unbearable *and* I need a lot of space to move between the ranges of deep emotional states. (You can read my "Both/And" poem on the next page.)

Jamie talked a lot about hearts. My favorite quote of his is, "Most people think the world is round, but it's really in the shape of a heart because it's God's heart," followed by, "God's heart is different colors and every color is a country." Perhaps that is why I continue to see it as a sign. His heart is shining in all the odd places hearts are found.

Others close to Jamie see them, too. In the 2021 holiday season, Jamie's big sissy found this heart-shaped potato in the bag she was about to mash.

It's amazing, the dimes, the butterflies, the hearts . . . the old avocado tree achieving new growth . . . And these signs keep coming, forever reminding me that Jamie is always around us. Each year between the anniversary of his passing and Jamie's birthday we hold a cleanup at the park that the community created to honor him at the street named after him (Jamie's Way). After all the hard work, we release butterflies in honor of his eternal presence. We love you always, Jamie. Mom loves you, son. We honor Jamie's life and legacy, and he continues to make a mark on this world.

Broken and Beautiful ("Both/And")

Written in memory of the 32 people who lost their lives in senseless violence on April 16, 2007 while trying to better themselves and the world.

Both/and
Broken and beautiful
Life is complex, spectacular, horrifying, scary, ugly, absolutely breathtaking, heartwarming, loving, hateful, wicked, amazing, inspiring, terrible, painful, completely astonishing, miraculous, evil, surprising, staggering, incredible.

I weep for the 32-plus-1
I wail for the 3,000-plus of 9/11
I sob even harder for the tens of thousands more dying in war
All forms of human atrocity
Spewed out daily on the radio, television and social media

Should I retreat in respite from the agony?
Should I flee into my own safe world?

Only my world is no more protected
It knows the deepest of grief
I've known for 5 years now what the parents of Virginia Tech
are just now discovering

Where, then, do I escape?
When my private experience mirrors the suffering of the world—
The deepest of losses
The most extreme of betrayals
Where is my innocence to be found?
How do I live the legacy?

It comes back again and again to this moment
The simple pleasure of touch
The uplift of sunrise
The connection to Spirit
and love of friends.

Yes I will keep breathing in the pain
and breathing out compassion
I will not apologize for that again
I will acknowledge the suffering
but enjoy the moment.
This is who I am
This is how I heal
This is my journey
In this broken and beautiful world

© Elene Bratton April 19, 2007

CHAPTER SEVEN

"How Are You?" and Other Loaded Questions

I t is well known to any grieving person that the world is ill equipped to deal with such deep feelings, but those who lose children cannot even be named. It's just too awful to mention.

Those who lose spouses are called widows and widowers, and those who lose parents are orphans. But parents who have lost children sometimes use the phrase "bereaved parents" to give themselves a name. Bereaved parents and others surviving loss have a double task: We must grieve and we must teach others how to support us in the grief process.

If we can't—or won't—we are far less likely to get the support needed to make it from *surviving* to *living*. I am not even trying to make it to "thriving." That shipped sailed on April 24, 2002. But living? Living life out loud? I can do that.

So what about all of the people we have to deal with while trying to make it from the "surviving" phase to the "living" phase? First, just know that this is the society we have, if you live in a modern Western culture. It is a western approach that believes in "polite" grieving. "Polite" grieving should last under a year and should mostly be done in silence, after your three days of bereavement leave—for immediate family only. We call this "grief illiteracy."

I must pause to again acknowledge Dr. Ken Druck, who taught me most of what was helpful to me in healing grief, and so much more. I experienced "grief illiteracy" long before Dr. Druck gave it a name. From previous losses, I had experienced society's lack of understanding grief and the bereaved, but those previous losses had never taken all of me. This loss was all consuming and left me unable to function or ward off unhelpful and unskilled attempts at "support."

In prior instances of grieving, I was able to recover among the "status quo" grieving processes and supports—which traditionally ended soon after the funeral. But the loss of my 5-year-old son required an entirely different scope of support: This time, my ability to keep living was more dependent on support from others—others who, by no fault of their own (I came to understand), just didn't know how to help. The issue lies squarely in our approach to dealing with feelings, especially ones so primitive as a loss this deep; the loss of a child. So, I had to search for what might work. I read about other cultures' grieving processes in books like Sukie Miller's "After Death: How People Around the World Map the Journey After Life," and "Finding Hope When a Child Dies, What Other Cultures Can Teach Us" by the same author, among others.

During numerous conversations with bereaved parents, attending countless hours of counseling and grief groups, reading grief books, and trusting my body to know how to grieve, I discovered the concepts I needed to help me carve out ideas and develop a way to find my own grieving path, have a deeper compassion for those in grief, forgive those who just didn't know, and ignite a passion in me to help our society learn how to grieve in healing ways. I hope that I will impact those on my path, including you, the reader, to develop a little more grief acumen.

Because we live in a grief-illiterate society and most people don't know what to say, it is no easy task to be among others while processing grief. People either say some cliché they've heard, which rings useless and hollow when you're in the grip of acute grief, or they shy away from you, afraid to say anything. Even more cruelly, they sometimes stay away or cross the street in order to avoid you.

So, these are the choices the newly-bereaved have to deal with in our culture: 1. You can let people know what you need, 2. You can suffer in silence, becoming more resentful until you just don't want to be around others, period, or 3. You can accept the limitations of being human. After Jamie left his body, I eventually chose 1 and 3. This is not to say that I never slip into 2 (suffering in silence, becoming more resentful). I just don't choose to stay there.

Ultimately, you are responsible for your healing. Getting mad at others because they don't know better, or aren't teachable, is a waste of your valuable energy. And you are going to need that precious energy to live again. At first, Mychael and I tried to help people understand what we needed. I mentioned earlier about our "Martin Luther" moment . . . along with our cussing-people-out moments. And these actions did help! A lot of our closer friends got it and really tried to be sensitive with their language, rote phrases and platitudes. But other times it wasn't worth it, especially if you didn't know the person well or wouldn't see them often.

Over time I have come to understand the limitations of human comfort and to forgive and accept that no one knows what to do in the face of such anguished pain in the eyes of another human being. Still, I have made it part of my healing mission to educate our society on how to deal with grief and those in grief. I have found that the more open I am about my grief process and talking about Jamie the more comfortable others will be in following suit.

What is okay. The thing the grieving person needs others to know, in order for the grieving person to feel safe with them, is that it is okay *to not be okay*. It is also okay to talk about the loved one who has passed away.

What is not okay. Consciously knowing that people are just being the way I *used to be*—"well-meaning" people, "don't mean to hurt you" people—doesn't make the clichés, platitudes and social greetings any easier.

It is important to have this safe outlet, as grief must be witnessed, pain must be seen, to begin to heal. Feelings must be allowed expression—from the absurd superstitions, such as believing some random past act (in my case, naming my son after my cousin Jamie who passed away at 21 years old in 1983 caused Jamie to be doomed to early death) to feelings that are expected, such as sadness, anger, guilt. All of these feelings must have another human to hear and hold, to know you are not going mad. The feelings of grief can be so profoundly deep that it feels like you are the only one who has ever thought or felt this way. You are not.

Take the customary greetings "Hi, how are you?" and "How ya doing?" and other forms of this highly-intrusive (to the bereaved) social greeting.

I mean it. *Take them, please!* Take them out of the lexicon.

I am on a one-woman campaign to do just that, and have written an essay in the following chapter on just how we can all be more sensitive to that.

In the meantime, here are key phrases I suggest you avoid:

"_____ is in a better place."

"_____ must be special, because God needed _____."

"_____ wouldn't want you to go around being sad/crying/angry, etc."

You don't know what the deceased want. Maybe they want to be greaved over. Who knows?

Even phrases referencing trauma, often casually with no intent attached, to this day, make me feel a horrific "pang"—phrases such as, "I must be brain-dead . . ." make me want to SCREAM, "That's how my son died!!!" Saying things are "dead," such as phones or watches, is also triggering. My son is dead. These devices just need to be recharged.

Removing militaristic and violent language from your speech such as, "silver bullet," "bullet points," "that's 'the bomb,'" can be helpful, too. You never know who may have lost someone in a shooting.

Overuse of extreme words of grief, like saying your day is "tragic" because you're having a bad hair day, or you "could've died" when you had an embarrassing moment are hard for those who grieve to bear.

I can't list every phrase here—and that would be unrealistic. I'm just trying to convey that it really does go a long way to be sensitive with your wording. There are many walking wounded, and the way we speak, with all of our violent references, can be hard on the bereaved.

This may be a time when my mom was right: "If you don't have anything good to say, don't say anything at all." However, this can hurt just as much, so I will rephrase: If you don't know what to say, ask, sit and listen, or do something else that might be useful such as bringing food, cleaning, shopping, offering to drive, etc. You'd be amazed at how everyday tasks are literally "too much" when grief strikes.

CHAPTER EIGHT

Do You Really Want To Know How I'm Doing?

———

"**H**ow are you?**"** is easy when you're doing great. It's like going to your high school reunion with a beautiful spouse, being president of your own company, driving a Rolls Royce and wearing a size 8. No problem! It's just those pesky times in life when we're, say, struggling—or had an unspeakable tragedy befall us.

I will concede to this: Part of the problem is that I can't really tell when someone is sincerely asking "How are you?" and wants an honest answer to the question or when it is simply part of a perfunctory social greeting. Sometimes it is easy to tell the difference, like when the person has physically kept moving—past you—by the time the question is completed. But other times it is not as clear whether the question is sincere, or if it is easy to answer in the time and place in which it is asked.

Hence the wondering posed in this chapter. How do we greet each other appropriately according to our social norms and how do we sincerely convey that we want to know how someone is doing? It would be great to find a new question we could pose when someone really wants to know. I would like to find a new phrase to be given as part of the greeting—if it is actually necessary to say more than "hello" or "Hi," which I would also argue it is not. ("Good Mornings" are often *not* "good" mornings, so I'd avoid that greeting, too.)

For a person who is not "fine" (which, by the way, the 12 step programs have defined as fearful, insecure, neurotic and emotional), the question itself is a struggle to endure. It is so overused that it is cliché, and to answer in the expected way causes the hurting person more pain. When the question is thrown out there by people who are simply doing their social duty and really don't want to know, it causes the person who isn't fine—sitting in refreshed anguish, taking stock of how they are really doing, while the average "how do you do" partner has whizzed on down the road—more injury.

Yes. It causes more injury. Why? The grieving individual will likely be put in the position of "failing to take care of the other person's feelings" because they seem "rude" for not participating in the social ritual, and the "inquiring" person ends up walking away in disgust. This only adds *shame* to the struggling individual's pain. Nice!

Sometimes, the question-asker has responded back to themselves by imagining your "fine" response, as you're asking yourself the same question within while *they* respond by telling *you* how *they* are doing. It goes something like this:

Q: "Hi, how ya doing?"

A: "Hello . . ." (thinking about the question)

Q: "I'm doing well, thank you. So, I wanted to know how that project is going (blah, blah, blah) . . ."

A: (still thinking, but trying to move on with the conversation) "I'm almost done . . ." (did you want to know how I am actually doing?)

Meanwhile, the person who is hurting is reliving all that has broken their heart (well, my child is sick, my mom died last week, I lost my job, I must have surgery on my knee—how do you think I'm doing?).

Some people will push you for an answer when you try to avert the question. They ask, "How are you?" and, being denied the "I'm fine" they are expecting, ask it again and again until you are forced to say something. Then they act like you are a really rude person if you let them know you don't care to discuss that with them.

Often, I've experienced these situations with complete strangers like store clerks and office receptionists who don't even know me and with whom I don't want to share, even if the question were sincere.

What makes the distinction important is that there are people who really want to know how a person is doing. But most people (at least I) can't tell who they are because the question-turned-greeting-phrase is so over used.

People who loved me and genuinely wanted to know how I was coping after the death of my son Jamie would ask me how I was doing, and I was so incensed by the question that both the sincere individuals and the ones who just wanted us to be okay so they could be comfortable would get the same response. I hurt several people, including my brother, because

I couldn't take the question. Even after all of these years it is difficult for me. Most every grieving person I know agrees; the question brings angst to an already difficult social environment.

I am advocating for a greeting that, rather than asks a question, makes a statement: "It's good to see you," "I'm glad you're here," "Glad you could make it," or even "What are you doing?" are all less intrusive and better tolerated. Or we could simply say "hello" and leave it at that.

You may be asking, "What if I am sincere and really want to know how someone is doing?" Here is what I suggest you do: Sit down with the person. Be with them. Acknowledge that you know things have been rough. Say something like, "I'm here and I'd really like to know how things have been for you."

The bereaved aren't the only ones who have trouble with the question "How are you?"

The poet Charles Bukowski says it this way in his poem:

problems in the checkout line

often in the supermarket checkout line

the cashier will ask me

"how are you?"

and I'll answer something

like, "not so good, I've got

hemorrhoids, insomnia, vertigo and

the battery in my watch is xxxx."

there's never a response, it's as if

they haven't heard, they just keep

ringing up my purchase.

I am not attempting to take out my

frustrations on the supermarket

employees

but when they ask me

"how are you?"

I'm usually not doing very well and there's nothing that

makes me feel worse

than to say

"fine."

I've tried another way.

when they ask

"how are you?"

I say, "it's never been so

good! it's unbelievable! the money's
just rolling in! I don't understand it!"

but they dislike this reply
more than the
hemorrhoid, insomnia, vertigo bit.

so I've tried a third way.
when they ask that same question I say,
"you really don't care."

again there's no reaction,
they just go on
ringing up my purchase
and I understand this lack of response:
they really don't care,
and I think that's good.
we all ought to realize that it's
nothing to be ashamed of
and it makes buying
groceries
the same as
anything else:
what we need is what we want and
what we want
has very little to do
with anything
else.

"How are you?" epitomizes the rote way we live and interact with one another. It's another way we keep our distance while *appearing* connected. I know it's a hard habit to break. It is such a part of our nomenclature that it is almost impossible not to say. It's such a part of our culture that preschoolers are taught songs on how to ask "how are you" and how to reply "fine." I must admit that it slips past my lips when I'm distracted, not present or caught off guard in a conversation.

I know many of you will be unable to change this habit. Jamie's dad thinks it is futile to even mention it and has succumbed to saying, "I'm hanging in there" or returning the question with another question such as, "What's happening?" or trying to move on to the next part of the conversation by simply ignoring it.

But since I'm swimming upstream anyway, I thought I'd try. Not so much to change our entire social language, but at least to make us reflect next time we ask the question, "How are you?"

grira sol

CHAPTER NINE

Life on Life's Terms

The Power of Radical Forgiveness

I t would be so nice, fair even, if there a was a loss quotient for each person, a point at which the Universe would say, "Enough is enough!" A line that wouldn't be crossed. An equal measure for each human heart. But, alas, life is less fair and more random in my experience.

Angela
◠•◡

After watching our son pass away, we rushed over to another hospital where my sister, Angela, was lying in an induced coma. As a result of the car accident, she had a massive head injury. We didn't know if she would make it. She did. While she was recovering, the doctor advised us against telling her about Jamie. We tortured ourselves for a month, making up stories about why he couldn't come visit, all the while wishing they were true and dying inside.

Her husband Jerry was by her side, for the first few months, but brain injury—also known as Traumatic Brain Injury (TBI)—is forever. It was a hard road, having to learn to walk, talk, and do for yourself all over again. She went home after approximately six weeks of rehabilitation. But she was different. She was very emotional, having to learn what the rest of us already knew. Also, she couldn't think quickly and no tasks were simple. Her emotions were very raw and close to the surface. She just wasn't her previous self. Jerry wasn't able to handle it, so he left.

She and her 10-year-old son, Demetri, couldn't care for themselves, so they moved in with us. This tested our conviction to forgive. Going from one hospital to the next was automatic for us. We knew we had to be there for Angela. But that doesn't mean it wasn't trying.

The detective who investigated the case told us even before the report's conclusion was finalized that there were only four causes for car crashes: A) driving under the influence, B) a malfunction of the car, C) a medical emergency with the driver, or D) distracted driving. A and B had been ruled out. And while I thanked the heavens for that, because if it had been something my sister caused by being drunk or loaded, I don't know that I would have been able to live with that. The report, which I still haven't been able to read, couldn't rule out a medical issue, because she had so many after the crash. Despite this, he concluded it was likely distracted driving, which had been my sense all along.

On day one, when I knew she was at fault, I made an immediate decision, based on who my sister is and her relationship with Jamie, that she would never do anything to intentionally cause him harm. She had taken time in her day to drive from La Costa to San Diego, in heavy traffic, to pick up her nephew to spend time with him and her son (his cousin), Demetri. The three of them were going to eat pizza and watch a movie and she was going to drive him back to school the next morning. That's love. Pure love. That's an admirable act, that most of us need to do more of, including myself. Understanding who my sister is and what her intensions were, I didn't feel anything but love for her.

That is not to say I didn't have dark thoughts at times. Thoughts I am ashamed to admit. "Why does she get to have her son when she was driving, and my son is gone?" "Why does she get to have a relationship, when my marriage ended because of her?" These thoughts became very inflamed when my sister shared with me some memories that she was finally able to bring to the surface.

After the accident, she racked her brain for years trying to remember anything about what happened. And an image finally came. She recalled her cell phone ringing, it was on the seat beside her, and as she reached to answer it, she recalled her strappy platform shoes coming loose and causing swerving. She stopped there, not wanting to see more.

I have to admit, that admission brought on a very powerful feeling of anger inside of me. I discussed it with close friends, and once again came back to the same place: My sister loved Jamie. She didn't know better at the time. Actually, none of us did. Driving while under the influence of a cell phone wasn't even illegal yet. It could just as easily have been me, if I had bothered to make the time to spend time with my nephew.

I can't say that the hurt and anger never get directed toward blaming her. But I *can* say that AA has taught me that, although we are not responsible for our thoughts, we are responsible for what we do with them. And when I do what I've done so far, I come back to the same conclusion. I love my sister and I am so glad she is still alive. If I had gotten to pick, of course I would pick Jamie, so would she, but I am so glad that I am not mourning both my sister and my son.

I know that day was preventable. She will always live with the guilt of her choice to reach for that phone, but she also lives with a brain injury. Two people I love were physical victims of the crash that day. Neither of them deserved it. We both agree, my sister and I, that if we can stop another person from such a tragedy by sharing our story, we will use our experience to benefit someone else. Sometimes that is all we can do, learn from our mistakes and do better. So, *do* I forgive my sister? I do. Yet I never had to "forgive" her, because I did not condemn her. Those who do not condemn, don't need to forgive. It is up to her to forgive herself, and I know that will be a lifetime process, just as it would be for any of us in the same situation.

Alexander

In 2002, the year our dear, sweet boy Jamie left his body, life continued to "show up." In September 2002, our family had been invited by a friend to stay at his cabin in Idyllwild for the weekend. I remember it being a bit rough for us—Mychael, me, my 20-year-old daughter Danielle, her 4-month-old son Raell, Jamie's 10-year-old cousin Demetri and my sister Angela. My daughter had bought a new Odyssey van that Wednesday prior. It was our first outing as a family since Jamie had left his body. We went to this beautiful place in the mountains, and we didn't know what to do with ourselves, so we came back a few hours early.

I remember my husband was sitting in the passenger seat and Danielle was driving. I was sitting in the back seat and baby Raell was next to me. Demetri and Angela were in the way back, napping on the way home. I remember Mychael reading a grief book out loud and us discussing it when I heard my daughter say, "What are they doing?" and then a loud "BAM!" When we stopped, the van was turned 360 degrees, but everyone was fine. Raell was screaming, but not physically hurt, and Demetri was crying.

It was so very hot out, a scorching fall day in the low desert. I took the kids and got us into the little bit of shade I could find. My husband was talking to some good Samaritans that stopped by. I could see my daughter climbing—through broken glass—into the back seat of the other car. My sister was talking to the driver. Soon the ambulances arrived and they were tending to us. I could see, from my cot in the back of my ambulance, as they shut the door, workers pulling up the sheet over a little boy's face. I screamed, "He's dead, he's dead!" My heart filled with dread and agony for this other family, who I knew would soon be making their decent into hell.

Only at the hospital would I learn that my daughter had sprained her ankle trying to apply the brakes to our vehicle, or that she had made her way into the back seat of the other vehicle, in an effort to give the boy CPR, while my sister stood at the window trying to comfort the mother. The crash was eerily similar to the one that had wreaked the same horror upon us only a few months prior. Another young boy taken, another family forever broken, another trauma leaving its mark on all involved.

But this tragedy came with a very strange twist. We were attending Compassionate Friends (TCF) regularly at the time, with the need never as strong as after being in a crash that killed another little boy. We were in the circle a few months after the crash, when a family came in and described their tragedy and gave the name of their lost little boy, Alexander Model Thomas. We had gotten his name and knew they were his kin. It was odd, but likely because our stories were so similar and close together, they were drawn to us. They came up to us after meetings to talk. We worried that if we revealed who we were they would not come back, and at this point we had to feel comfortable attending these meetings, too, as it was also our lifeline, so we didn't say anything.

After a few months of this, including the annual candle lighting where we see all our kids in a slide show, and upon seeing their beautiful boy's picture, we couldn't stand it anymore. We had to tell them. Mychael drafted and sent them a letter. We told them our story and how intimately our lives were entwined. We invited them over to talk with us, and they accepted. We readied ourselves that night, not knowing if they were coming to kill us or to find some healing. It was going to be just Alex's father and his parents. (The mother had been driving and was found at fault for the crash.) As it turned out, well, since I am writing this story many years later— they obviously did not kill us.

It is just so strange. Life's "rhyme and reason." We all had experienced the biggest tragedy to befall a family, and Mychael and I were put there, with them, to offer some comfort by sharing those last moments of *their* boy's life, subsequently united with them via a strange twist of fate as we all sought healing at those Compassionate Friends meetings.

Ashani

As the year was about to turn from 2002 to 2003—the first year in which Jamie would not exist in any part, which was heavy on our heart—we received another blow. Jamie's little "cousin," Ashani Samea Riley, who is the daughter of my daughter's best friend Chelees (and now, officially, *our family*, see below*), had contracted a rare cancer called rhabdomyosarcoma. She was such a fighter. No matter how hurt her already petite body was, she was brave and sweet in the face of it all. She fought for two years, she won for two years, and it came back and took her a final time after a valiant one-year fight. On March 9, 2008, Ashani Samea Riley, who I call my "Grand," joined Jamie in leaving her body and living forever in our hearts. (*I officially adopted Chelees at the end of 2021, with a new birth certificate and everything. This also expands our family with a new grandson, Jake, who was born in 2013.)

A Family Devastated

Death took our precious boy from us

But it did not stop there

In the guilt of grief, an auntie fled

In the anger of grief, a sissy hid

In the sadness of grief, a mommy slid into isolation and then depression

In the fear of grief, a daddy drifted suddenly away

One by One

And each for our own reasons

We scattered to the winds

The warmth of our home became just the space of a house

The bond of our love just a memory

It should be enough to lose such an integral part of our family

But to lose each other

The tragedy persists

Finding a means to absorb all the ways loss has demanded its due

Believing again in life and in each other

That is the prayer and hope of my heart

Perhaps

One by One

And each walking our path of healing

We will turn to the legacy left by our precious boy

and become a family connected by love, centered in peace and ready to

claim the joy of one another.

© Elene Bratton 1/21/06

A Family Devastated

Somewhere in the cloud of grief and trauma, several of my family members succumbed to the relief that substances promise to bring. I could see my daughter slipping away after the crash that killed Alexander Model Thomas. Danielle had tried so hard before "that day" to work as a certified nursing assistant, and she had graduated just weeks before Jamie left. She had baby Raell to think of, who was born on May 13, 2002, three weeks after Jamie's passing—and exactly six years from Jamie's original due date. She was going to counseling and groups, trying so hard to be there and walk through it all. But after the crash in Idyllwild, all that fell away. She became isolated and started numbing herself; just marijuana at first, but soon I saw another side that could only be one thing: Meth. It was ugly and painful to see it happening and not be able to stop it or even blame her for wanting the comfort the drug swore would be hers.

My sister's decline was subtler. She had moved out about two years after Jamie's accident, wanting her adult self back. She was so affected by the brain injury that it was hard to discern the truth of her decline. She was stating she was clean and sober, even going to 12 step meetings and claiming clean time. She always participated with the family and stayed connected, making it harder to see. But eventually, it all came crashing down on both my daughter and sister.

My husband's departure was the hardest to see coming. We had been closer after losing Jamie. It seemed that our mutual devastation had driven us to be more vulnerable with each other, to cling closer, to hold on tighter. I trusted so completely that we would be there for each other that I completely missed the signs. Then, all of a sudden, they were painfully clear. And it was too late. Although his body was still there, he was gone. All the previous adhesive that had kept us together for 14 years was dried up and no longer working. Right before Thanksgiving in 2005, about two and a half years after we lost our son, we lost each other.

For a long time I couldn't talk about him or to him. I was so overwhelmed by yet another deep loss, that I really just wanted to curl up and die. But thank the Universe I have great girlfriends. They wrapped around me and helped me breathe. I found new passions and eventually opened up to romance once more. It is a slow healing process, for this loss is similar, but with nuanced differences. I have no place to take this loss whereby I feel I can make a difference from it, or make meaning out of it. I felt stuck for a long time, but it's evolved from hurt and anger to recognizing, as family friend Karl Anthony said in one of my all-time favorite "reminder" songs, "It's Only Change"—*It's only change in my life, it's alright, it may rearrange, but its only change.**

Mychael and I can now discuss organizational needs for Jamie's Joy, and sometimes we even share a memory of the sweet boy we brought into the world. The "how" may have been hard, but I am happy living my life as an independent single woman answering only to myself and the legacy of the Bratton clan. And besides, everyone needs an area to work on. Otherwise, why be a human on earth, if we have it all figured out and under control?

After her fall, Danielle had a hard time being stable. She was renting rooms which could easily be taken from her, and, fortunately,

---

*"It's Only Change" by Karl Anthony © circa 1992.

during the downturn in the economy, I was able to purchase a condo for her to lease. During this time, she had a second son, named Isaiah Jamie, in 2010. Unfortunately, in 2011, my daughter lost her kids to CPS. But Danielle is one of the rare parents I've seen rally when this happens. I've observed many more fall into despair, never to reclaim their children or themselves. But, alas, that is a topic for another book. She has worked so hard to get, and stay, clean. She went through a program called Vista Hill ParentCare and became part of the alumni group. She did so well that she was hired at the facility where she got sober and still works there to this day. Since then, she also had a baby girl, Destiny Ashani.

My sister finally admitted to herself, and then to us, that she hadn't been clean all those years. Now she not only attends but truly participates in meetings and works a program. Even my son-in-law, Antonio—never wanting to be outdone—got in on the act! My brother Alexis is on what's called the harm reduction plan but it is working for him. He has been with us in San Diego for several years now. Prior to that, I hadn't been around him consistently since living at home in my teens. Lastly, my nephew (and Jamie's "brother"), Demetri, is now a man. He has a lovely family (a wife and two kids), and though I know growing up with this tragedy wasn't easy, he seems pretty well adjusted.

My "other daughter" Chelees has had another child, named Jake. ("From State Farm" as we like to call him.) He is totally different from his sister, Ashani. He knows Ashani and Jamie, and asks lots of questions. His outgoing personality, innate sense of humor, curiosity and intelligence remind me of Jamie. And even though some have gone and others are always missed, we have cobbled together a lot of love, despite knowing it can be taken again at any time.

I am so grateful for the power of healing that has increased in my life during this tragedy. My belief in this power has strengthened, and, while these tragedies will always be extremely tender, I know that Spirit is Love and Spirit is Healing, and that Spirit has touched us all—in different moments and different ways. It is not a straight course, but deeply and profoundly it is witnessed by our survival and willingness to keep moving forward.

I share this part of my story in hopes that you will be gentle and compassionate with yourself and your family as your grieve, as we all absorb losses and heal at our own pace and in our own time.

Azim

I would be remiss, in a chapter that includes radial forgiveness, if I did not mention my forgiveness guru, Azim Khamisa. Azim's son Tariq was shot by a 14-year-old boy named Tony Hicks who was trying to "jump" (initiate) into a gang. Tony was tried, convicted and sentenced to 25 years to life in 1995. At the time, he was the youngest person in California to be tried as an adult. Instead of holding hate in his heart for the young man, Azim had the wisdom to realize there were victims on both sides of that gun. He advocated for Tony and remained in contact with him during his incarceration.

Azim also founded the Tariq Khamisa Foundation in honor of his son, devoting himself to peaceful conflict resolution through a restorative justice model. But he didn't stop there: He invited Ples Felix, Tony's grandfather, to join him. Together they work to bring this program into middle schools in order to help young kids make different choices. They speak together to show others the power of forgiveness. They've been working together for over 25 years, and in 2020, when Tony Hicks was released from custody, he was welcomed into the organization. Now all three of these men tell their story of radical forgiveness, ever reminding me that there's nothing, absolutely nothing, in this world that I can't forgive.

"When you forgive, your heart stays pure,
and love is able to flow."

I may not do it as gracefully as Azim, and it may take a longer time and be a more intense process, but if Azim can do it, so can I. Forgiveness is not for the person that's forgiven but for the forgiver. When you forgive, your heart stays pure, and love is able to flow. A hardened heart also hardens to the good things. I leave my heart open to feel Jamie, to stay connected to family and friends, and yes, that can leave me vulnerable to more hurt and heartache, but I am *already guaranteed* that outcome if I *can't* feel love, joy, peace & connection, so I'll take my chances on forgiveness.

CHAPTER TEN

My Utopian Vision

S o, here's my utopian fix for all of life's losses and traumas:
We all just expire at midnight on our 70th birthday. We can
spend that day in the way we enjoy most, surrounded by loved ones,
in solitude, having a group send-off or alone under the stars.

We choose. It's our day, and we can't die a moment sooner or later. But
who would want to, because most of the causes of our suffering are gone.

There's no way to die from accident, injury or illness. No one can kill
you and you can't kill yourself. No murder, nobody dies too young, no
suicide, no gnarly accidents, no war where we kill each other, no famine,
no natural disasters, no lingering illness that drains you of life before fin-
ishing you off. Just a day that's 70 years after you're born. Our bodies are
worn, but not too old where they're worn out. And not so young that we

don't get to live all the natural cycles. And while I know that as long as I am still not in charge of the Universe this isn't likely to happen, it makes me feel better to fantasize this world where Jamie would still be here, and no parent would outlive their child, and no child would grow up with their parents dying when they are young. (The current life expectancy is 70.2 years, so we're getting pretty close, anyway!)

Okay, back to reality.

Yes, it would be nice if life weren't so randomly cruel and hideously unkind, or at least a little bit fairer, but life appears as it does and we will experience death whenever it comes. When I get too down, I think of the Kennedys and how they suffered the horror of loss of the best and brightest of their clan over and over, and how Abraham Lincoln lost almost every political race he entered before becoming one of the most beloved presidents—the one that saved our union and ended slavery. But he was not spared: He, too, lost a son. And this all reminds me that no one gets through life unscathed. I don't know why, but that brings me comfort as well. As the saying goes, "It's not how many times you fall down, it's how many you get up again.

I'd like to say that I am always graceful about getting back up. I am not. Sometimes I still feel like life is a domestic violence relationship where instead of telling me to get out, everyone wants me to stay. So, stay I do, but not without angst or the impending feeling of doom that I might just get knocked down once more.

"Did you know we all live in God's heart?"

—Jamie, 5 years old

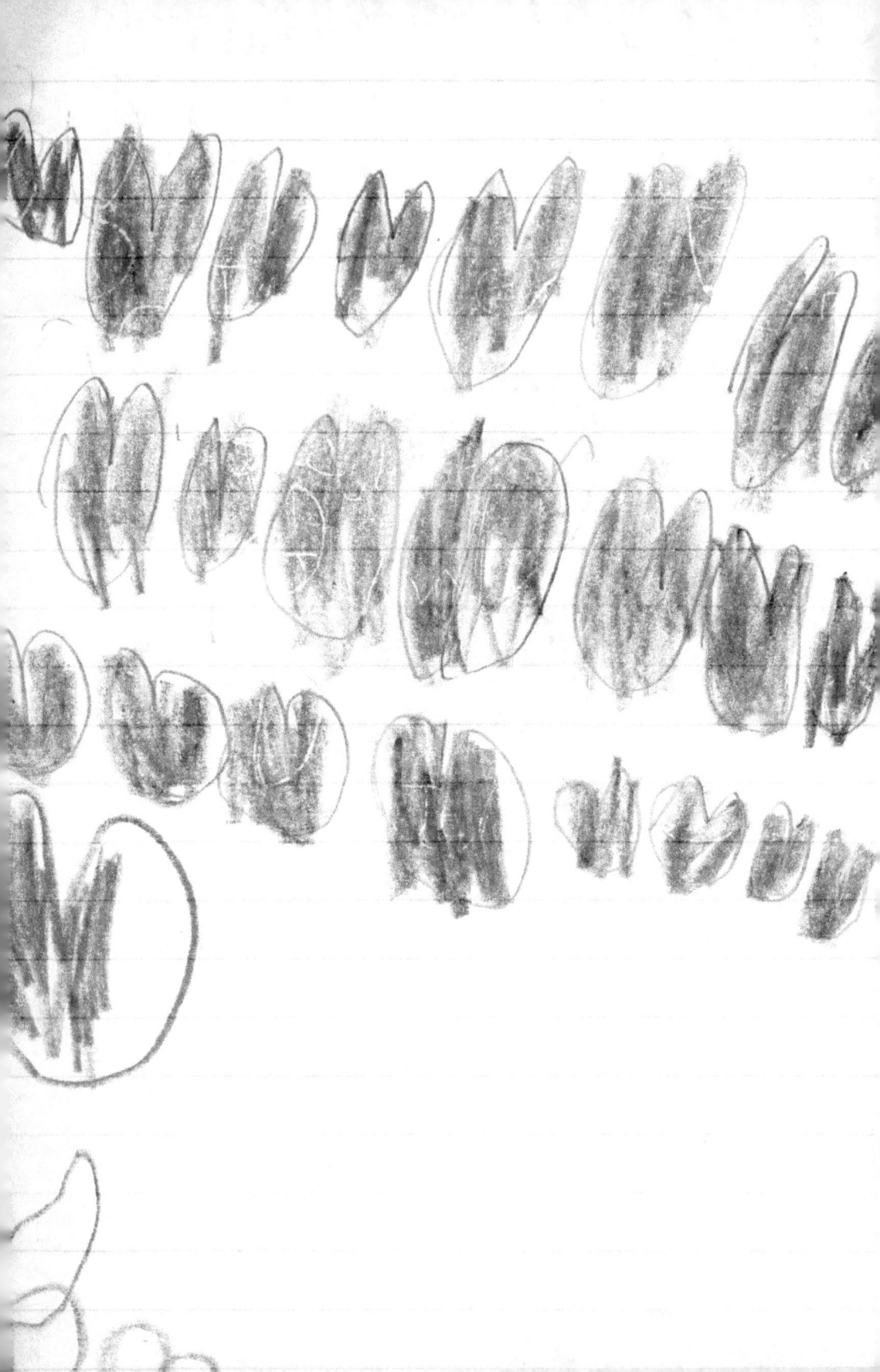

CHAPTER ELEVEN

Staying Connected with the Next Generation

D o you believe in a space between death and life where souls can meet? I believe in such a place, and it brings me comfort in the face of feeling hopeless.

Raell & Jamie

My 19-year-old daughter Danielle was in her last month of pregnancy with Raell when Jamie left his body on April 24, 2002. She gave birth to Raell on May 13, 2002, with the help of my first son-in-law, Ralph—six years to the day of Jamie's original due date of May 13, 1996—and just three weeks after Jamie had left his body.

Although Danielle's pregnancy had been an initial shock and source of concern for me and my husband, it had been a delight and source of pure joy for Jamie. Little five-year-old Jamie was so excited for the new baby to come! He wanted to be an uncle so badly, he could *hardly wait*—and maybe he didn't have to.

Raell started life in an environment of deep grief out of the ashes of the two tragic car accidents in 2002. Jamie's dad Mychael, my daughter Danielle (and, hence, Raell), my sister Angela (also in the crash with Jamie; almost died and left with a TBI) and her son Demetri and I all lived together for the first two years after Jamie's passing. As I grew close to "Rae," I developed a deep sense that Jamie and Raell met and came to know each other in the "space between"— the time when both were in between worlds. I can't ever prove this but it seemed like he and Jamie met in the Spirit world during the three weeks after Jamie left his body and before Raell was born into his.

Raell is a very dark-complected boy, who had light blond curly hair when he was very young which looked a lot like Jamie's. Much like Jamie, he also loved nakedness and whole vegetables when he was little.

He was very connected to Jamie as a child. He would talk to him and about him, even getting jealous or mad at him, showing a strong and complicated relationship. He received a lot of Jamie's old clothes, blankets and toys, which allowed me to hand down some of the material possessions with the reassurance that they weren't too far away. But it was more than just "stuff." I could sense they had a connection.

My daughter gave Raell Jamie's name as a middle name. She did the same for her second son, Isaiah. Her daughter Destiny has

Ashani as a middle name, in honor of our adoptive family member Chelees's daughter Ashani (my "Grand"), who also tragically passed on as a young child.

Below is an article I wrote after taking the Grands to see the play Jamie and I missed:

The Circle of Life
by Elene Bratton

In 2002, my family had made plans to visit Jamie's cousin Ari, who was about one at the time, in New York. Jamie was really into the Lion King, which had come to Broadway. We made plans to see it while in the city. Unfortunately, that was not to be, but 14 years later the play had made it to San Diego. When my friend Ronda asked me if I wanted to go with her, I had to take pause. Was I ready? I said yes, but only if I could take my grands (grandchildren), Destiny who was 4 and Isaiah who was 6, with us. I intuitively felt that, if I could complete this journey with them and come full circle in healing this one section of the grief experience, I would get a do over.

Ronda was very generous and courageous as she listened to my history with this play. Months had passed since we made that plan, but unlike the past, the day did arrive, with not a lot of thought but openness to what it might be. I arrived with all the stress of parking, fighting off throngs of ushers that want to direct you to your seat and settling the kids in.

I was prepared to feel sad about the journey that was thwarted by life all those years ago, but what I didn't remember was how much the story reflected my journey of love and loss. As the animals presented themselves in the Circle of Life, the tears started to flow as I realized I was fulfilling that circle in my own life through the connection to legacy in these moments I shared with my grands.

As I saw Mustafa instructing his son on the ways of the world, I remembered giving Jamie such instruction. It also triggered a memory of Raell as a baby, and holding him up in the air to survey his kingdom (only the backyard, but hey, it's what we've got).

When Mustafa was tragically killed, of course I plunged into my own sense as loss and grief. How suddenly you can go from feeling on top of the world, that life just keeps getting better and better, to questioning everything: purpose, meaning, faith, even the value of living and how loss lowers your sense of self in an instant. But running away, as Simba did, and so many do, simply doesn't work. Grief will wait in the darkness and find you when you are most vulnerable. Your attempts to run will have to be more intense and stronger until the medicine you seek to forget and comfort kills more than just the pain; it strangles out joy, all life and all hope of healing.

What has worked for me is to remember that we Inter-are, meaning, always connected: I am Jamie, Jamie is me; we literally share the same

DNA. We can never be separated. When Simba asks Rafiki (the wise monkey narrating the story), "Did you know my father?" He replies, "Correction: I know your father." This moved me so, causing me to reaffirm that what I know must be practiced. As much as I know the Spirit of Jamie lives on in me, I also have to practice seeing him, and his legacy of Love*Joy*Peace*Connection. That is how I keep him alive in me. For a long time, Simba couldn't feel the continuation because he couldn't let go of his guilt in order to connect with the presence of his father, and feel how his father was in him and he was in his father. We remain connected even if our bodies are apart.

It was beautiful to see the Lion King story reflecting the approach I have taken in channeling my grief through service. Once he felt that connection, he went back to his community to help. That is what we have with Jamie's Joy. That is what I do each time I open my heart wide to love again, to spending time with my family, my future, my grands, my community, my life. By continuing to be in the Circle of Life I not only honor the life of my son, but the whole of life.

Edited and Printed in the City Beat by Thom Senzee, April 2014

The circle does continue. Life does move on. And that both hurts *and* heals. As time passes, kids grow, their interests change, they make their own friends, and so I have to make the time to keep that connection strong with all of my loved ones, friends and family. We make time for family trips, carve out special occasions for gathering, but what I cherish most are the times I get to hang out, go to the beach, climb a tree, read a book together or play "lava rock" or "alien abduction" (a scary version of "Hide and Seek") with them.

I now have four living official grands and a gaggle of kids who call me "grammy"—basically that's my name to all kids I meet—and when I'm with them, I'm a kid, too. Our most recent addition is Dylan (Aizen's brother), born to Demetri Weir and Jen Quach, and James (Devon's brother), born to Lyric and Malcolm (who left his body in December, 2022), who is named after Jamie by one of Jamie's closest childhood family friends.

The article below also shows how I've created that sense of continuity amid the grief, and gives you a sense of how Jamie's Joy organization came to be:

Living Life Out Loud— Oh The Places We'll Go.

Jamie's Joy as an organization has been an outlet for sharing Jamie and channeling our grief.* It has had many incarnations. I shared its inception and Jamie's spiritual guidance that has led us. I think anyone who has lost someone, especially a young person, needs to find that person's legacy to and for them. Sometimes it is very clear because the person had a passion. Jamie was very young, and although a clear zest for life was present, a passion hadn't yet blossomed. We didn't set out to find his legacy, we just knew we wanted to create something that would last past a one-time giving. And we know Jamie. "Joy" was easy to see. The Love, Peace and Connection came from thinking about who he was and hearing how he touched and left a lasting impression on all with whom he interacted.

On Jamie's 6th birthday, just a month after the crash, we had what ended up becoming our first Jamie's Joy event. Karl Anthony played music which included two songs he had written in the aftermath of Jamie's passing. We had information tables on grief at the event. North County Hospice provided trained workers to help the kids (of all ages) process their feelings.

---

*See "About Jamie's Joy" at the end of this book.

Looking back, I have no idea how we did that. But it started something. It started Jamie's Joy. In 2003–2007 we did letter writing campaigns and asked friends and family to support an organization we thought embodied Jamie's Spirit. For the next 10 years we held community events that involved the organization for which we were raising funds, including local dignitaries and media coverage, and raised tens of thousands of dollars. Every year we choose organizations that served the age Jamie would be, many of which we continue giving to annually through Jamies Joy.

It has always felt to me as if Jamie is aging. It is one of the greatest sadness's that I don't know what Jamie would look like, be interested in, be up to as he got older. Would he be gay, straight, bi or transgender? Would he be away at college, or smoking pot in my basement? Would he still have long hair? Would it have darkened over time? Would he know Spanish or play an instrument, be into art or science, maybe both?

Even with not knowing the answers to these and so many more questions, one thing I did know (that intuition thing again) was that he wouldn't want to keep having this big party after the big twenty-one. He was grown up now.

With that, Jamie's Joy has shifted to being more about service. It is my goal that we create avenues for people to serve where Love*Joy*Peace*Connection are alive. And to create joyful memories and fun adventures for folks who want to serve as part of their passion. I call it "Living Life Outloud." It means being with others, making a difference where you are and where you go, it means taking a stand for justice, caring and compassion. It means breathing in the pain and breathing out the love. It means living life to the fullest, no regrets, keeping our hearts open, loving hard, continuing to be involved, "a part of," helping each other and pushing ourselves further than we think we can go. Once we've faced the worst, the rest is a piece of (birthday) cake.

One thing I have realized as I have served through Jamie's Joy is I don't have to invent everything myself. There are plenty of organizations that have the structure. I can simply show up and invite others to do the same. Together we can make a difference not only in our local, national and international communities but in ourselves. If you want to join me, find me. My contact information is listed at the front and back of this book. If you have someone for whom you need to carry on a legacy, find what you both can be passionate about and live that life within your own. In this way I hope we both find the peace and healing we are seeking on our journeys.

Until we meet, keeping trudging the road of healing.

JAMIE's Self Portrait

CHAPTER TWELVE

Memories

"Jamie-isms"

Words and phrases. A child's words and phrases express the innocence and straightforward nature of their thinking at different ages. From the time Jamie was three years old, he had much to say and much to teach. Some words and phrases Jamie used when he was first learning to speak. Some developed as he worked to build his mind and his understanding of the world. Some were left over from his first language, Spanglish. Here are some of our favorites.

"Bad cat chasing a mouse"
—Tom and Jerry cartoon

"The shows in between the shows"

—commercials

"5 minutes and 5 minutes and 5 minutes"

—how long until Sponge Bob is on.

"1:12 or 9:12"

—the answer to, "What time is it?"

"Agua melon"

—watermelon

"Brekfisk"

—breakfast

"Kid meat"

—vegetarian meat product

Rah-rahs

—monsters

"Broom-brooms"

—cars

"Bite"

—"I want something to eat"

"Shiggs"

—dogs (after Jiggs his dog)

"Shiggs ona doe"

—"Jiggs (the dog) wants to go with us"

"Academia nuts"

—Macadamia Nuts

"Lovenen, Kissenen, Missesen each other"

—loving, kissing, missing each other

"Fur-fur-fur"

—refrigerator

"Shyer"

—shower

"Oatmuhl"

—oatmeal

"Go Loud"

—"Speak louder please, I can't hear you."

"It fun"

—"I'm having fun"

"Gril, wirld, Cralos, Crambia"
—anything with a vowel and an "r" got switched (Karl Anthony became "Kral Antie")

"Tuley"
—kids older than him. He began calling his cousin Cody "Tuley" at age two and extended the name to include all kids a few years older than him

"I wanna jale your pelo"
—"I want to hold your hair" (used as a comfort when going to bed at night)

"Helmom"
—helmet

"Upstirs/downstirs"
—upstairs/downstairs

"Asking Marks"
—questions marks

"Explanation points"
—exclamation points

"Mote Trol"
—remote control

People think the world is round, but it is really in the
shape of a heart, because it's God's heart.

—Jamie, 5 years old

Feliz

Cumple-
años

te quiere
mucho
Jamie

CHAPTER THIRTEEN

Memories
From Jamie's Community of Love

—————

From Jamie's Mom and Dad
∽•∾

Last Five Days with Jamie In His Body
By Elene and Mychael

MOM: Friday, I got home early after a meeting that took me away from my office. Before leaving the hospital where the meeting was held, I donated some blood. When I got home, Myke and Jamie were out, so I went to the Chinese acupuncturist for the first time. When my boys got home, we needed to decide who was going to craft night. Jamie was all ready to go and I was gathering my photos to work on an album of Jamie. Myke was undecided, and then chose to stay home for some down time, so Jamie and I headed out to Ruth's house to meet up with the crafting gang. I had packed his P.J.'s and toothbrush, which became a routine for these late nights, as it is hard to wake Jamie once he falls asleep in the car.

We arrived at craft night to find Ruth had a great spread of veggies, pizza and desserts. As Jamie made his plate, Dr. Dixon asked, "Where's your protein?" (I would later find out this is an old family joke. Jamie pointed to the cookies.) As he watched a movie with Katie, Lucas and the other older kids, I proudly showed off his baby pictures. (Although he was not much older than a baby at this point, he liked to think of himself as a big boy. I indulged him by calling all his photos under four "baby pictures.") We also had a secret agreement that, although he is a "big boy," he will always be my baby.

At the close of the evening, I had about two pages of the album complete. Both Jamie and I brushed our teeth and changed into our pajamas before leaving Ruth's. He was asleep when we got home, and I carried him to bed, his teeth already brushed.

DAD: This was the day I went to pick Jamie up from school unannounced. When I arrived at the office to let them know I was there, one of the gals in the office said, "Oh, you must have gotten the message."

"No," I replied, "What message?"

"Hang on just a minute," she said, and walked into the vice principal's office. Emerging a minute later, she asked me if I could come back and talk to Viola, the VP. I somewhat reluctantly sauntered to her office, trying to imagine what had happened.

Viola sat me down and said, "Jamie mooned a couple of girls in class today."

"OK," I offered sheepishly.

"Well, I brought him in and we talked," the vice principal continued. "I asked him if he knew the difference between right and wrong. He said 'yes,' he did. I asked him then if what he did was right or wrong. He said it was wrong. Since he knew it was wrong, I didn't keep him any longer, but I did say he'd have to miss recess on Monday and Tuesday and spend that time in my office."

"That sounds fair," I agreed.

"You know, the funny thing is, when I asked Jamie where he learned to moon like that, he said he learned it from you."

I became flushed and tried to calmly explain that there were some things that we did at home, "mooning" people or peeing in the back yard, for instance, that I would tell Jamie were not appropriate in public. "Maybe I forgot to mention that particular act as being inappropriate," I admitted.

She looked at me as if she expected me to defend myself. I had no defense, so she let me go with no punishment. I went out to sit on the picnic tables and wait for class to get out. I kept my eyes to myself, imagining disgusted passersby looking over to see the guy who teaches his son to moon people. "What other things will he teach him?" I guessed at their thoughts.

When Jamie's class got out, I walked over the get him. Bree Anna, who was like the 5-year-old Class Mother, told me right away, "Jamie did something bad today."

"I know, Bree Anna, I will talk to him about it."

Jamie and I embraced, and as we walked holding hands to the parking lot, I asked him about the incident, sort of matter-of-factly. When we got in the truck, I told him, "Jamie, you embarrassed me."

"Why?" he asked.

"You told the vice principal that I taught you how to moon."

"Well, you did, Dad."

"I know," I replied. "But you didn't have to tell her that." I could hardly be mad at him. I was, after all, the one who needed to learn something more than he did.

MOM: Saturday morning we went on a hike with the "Happy Hikers" from the free spirits group through church. We were to follow the guided presentation about the flora and fauna of the landscape. Our group was small, so a troupe of boy scouts joined us. Jamie and I quickly got bored. Using Jiggs the dog as an excuse, we kept venturing ahead, only to be scolded by the group leader when we returned.

Finally, we made a clean break from the group and headed for the San Diego River. Jamie found some cool moss in the small swamp that passes as a river in the Mission Trails area. He asked and was granted permission to take off his shoes, socks and shirt. (Nature Boy was getting too shy to go down to his underwear or beyond anymore.) When the group caught up with us, we were having a great time playing swamp monster with the moss and enjoying the warm sunshine and cool water. The boy scouts weren't allowed to remove any articles of clothing so Jamie quickly began entertaining them by chasing them with the moss. We followed the group out at the end of the day, hiking rocks and trees along the way.

Sunday, Myke and I went to the gym. Jamie stayed with Sissy to get ready for church. We were all meeting at the church for Tayo's christening. Danielle, Jamie and I left the service at 10:30 am to head to Unity Church where I was teaching Sunday school for Jamie's class. Danielle was to help out in the nursery. As it turned out, the nursery was empty and I needed an assistant. Danielle helped in the 3 to 5-year-old classroom. We had a great lesson on caring for others. Jamie had a little tantrum but was able to rejoin the class for playtime with Play-Doh.

After church, we went into Wrigley Hall to buy some scrip and hit up some folks for the March of Dimes walk. Jamie saw they were having Sunday brunch—complete with strawberry pancakes. He wanted to eat. I explained to him we were meeting friends (Tayo and the christening party) for brunch. Being unsure of the menu, however, I couldn't promise him pancakes. The tears and Tantrum #2 began. I was so happy when we got to the restaurant and, not only did they have pancakes—they had waffles, too. Jamie ate and had a great time playing with the children and taking photos with Merlin.

His last photo was taken that day. Looking at it now, he looks so sure, so confident, so big.

DAD: Jill and Kevin had been holding our wedding present for about a year, and Kevin had brought it that Sunday. It was a beautiful ceramic angel, and a nice piece for our meditation garden.

MOM: Monday night, Myke and I both got home around 6:30. It was a nice night and it was staying light later. We decided to take a family walk around our neighborhood. With Jiggs in tow, we began. A few blocks down, we stopped at what used to be a friend's house. They hadn't lived there in a year and a half. We met a new fellow and drank some of his water.

Jamie was quite interested in his tree in the front yard, a Crista-Galli Coral tree. He asked if he could climb it. "No. I am just a renter and would not want anything to happen to you on the property," said the new neighbor.

"It is a weak-wooded tree," Myke added.

The neighbor's door shut and as we walked past the tree, Jamie grabbed onto it and swung back and forth. "Jamie, what are you doing? We just told you not to climb that tree!" we yelled simultaneously, shocked by the defiance.

"You said I couldn't climb on it, you didn't say I couldn't swing on it," was his logical, well thought out, and honest, answer. (I told that story to the Anger Management group the next day as an example of how specific and clear we must be in our communication if we are to get what we want!)

Tuesday afternoon, I got a call at work from Angela. She stated she had the next day off and wanted to "kick it with her nephew." I said I'd talk to Myke and get back to her.

Tuesday night I got home around 5:30. I went to get Jamie, who was playing at Taylor's. He was out front with his kite. I told him I thought they wanted him to leave it at their house but he insisted it was O.K. to take it home. He won. Home with the kite we went. It was trash night (Jamie's job, with my help). I was prompting Jamie when he announced loudly and proudly, "First I got to go poop!" Once done, he exited the bathroom with trash in hand. "Did you wipe?" Mom asked. "I forgot!" and assumed the position (a yoga, down-dog stance perfect for wiping). Mom wiped and then went to flush. Sitting in the toilet was the biggest poop (at least two feet!) I've ever seen. "How does such a big poop come from such a little boy?" I asked. "I don't know," Jamie replied, bouncing away with his trash.

Later, after trash was out and hands were washed, we sat to eat at the kitchen table. I made spaghetti and Jamie had some leftovers as well. Before I could talk to Myke or say anything to Jamie about my earlier conversation with Angela (I had actually forgotten), Jamie said to me, "I want to see my auntie and my Demetri." It was about 7:30 p.m. I then discussed it with Mychael over the phone. He thought it would be okay. So I called Angela to talk with her about the arrangements. Jamie and Demetri talked for a while on the phone.

It was settled. Jamie was going to spend the night at his Auntie's on Wednesday. She would pick him up at 3:30 pm from school and bring him back to school at 8:30 am on Thursday.

After dinner, and when Dad got home, we all settled in for the night. Jamie's homework assignment was to learn about exclamation points and questions marks through reading a story and pointing them out. We read **A Visit to The Haunted House**, a Hallmark pop-up book by Dean Wally. There were lots of exclamation points and a few question marks. Jamie kept referring to them as "explanation points" and "asking marks." He asked to "jale" my "pelo" (pull, or hold onto, my hair in Spanglish) before bed and I, of course, obliged. It was our special bonding time before bed.

DAD: Wednesday morning, I got up early as always (around 4:30 am) and thought I should wake Jamie up for breakfast, especially this morning since he'd be at Auntie's tonight. I went downstairs and got really close to his sleeping face. "Jamie, wanna get up and have oatmeal with your daddy?" This was a magical way to get Jamie up. He was an incredibly sound sleeper, but any mention of breakfast and he'd hop joyfully, eyes half shut, out of bed. He followed me upstairs, and sat down at the breakfast table. I heated water, and made oatmeal for both of us. This was a special time for Jamie and me. We did it a couple of times a week on average.

Usually, he would sit and eat, and I would stand at the counter and eat. That day, I decided to sit down, and we enjoyed our oatmeal together. We talked a little about the upcoming day, and about how he'd have to get a "green" at school so he could go with his auntie that evening. After breakfast, Jamie and I went back downstairs, and he climbed back into the nice warm bed next to Mommy. I kissed him and hugged him and we told each other how much we love each other, and I said goodbye to Jamie for the very last time.

MOM: Wednesday morning, April 24, 2002, started out as most of our weekdays do. I got up at 6:30 and did yoga for 20 minutes. Jamie's clothes were picked out. He would wear his Scooby Do overalls and brown hiking boots. I then went to the bed and stared down at the beautiful son and soul before me. Reading the words of his pajamas, I began to wake him by asking, "Are you Anakin Skywalker?"

His little head and curls nodded a firm "No."

"Are you my Jamie Lou?" A nod of the head confirmed this

identity. "Are you my big boy?" Another nod "Yes" again, and he was almost awake.

One eye popped open and the question meant to steal a few more minutes of sleep came: "Mom if I promise to keep my eyes open can I stay laying down during the prayers?"

"Okay, honey, but if your eyes close you have to sit up."

We said our prayers, brushed our teeth, and washed our faces. Jamie had a little accident in his Pull-Ups, which he still wore nightly for just such happenings. We washed his privates and he dressed, as he often did, watching Zoboomafoo on "KPDS" as he called it. We took his other, bigger, blue backpack for his trip to Auntie's tonight. We drove to Goya's, the neighbor and her family who watched him in the mornings and walked him to his bus stop. I told Goya, in my broken Spanish, that Jamie wouldn't be there on Thursday because he would be going to Auntie's for the night. Jamie was out of the car and at my window for a kiss.

I remembered I had forgotten to insert Day Four of eye drops for pink eye. He leaned over my lap in the car and I put the drops carefully in his eyes. He got up and we embraced and kissed again. The last embrace, the last kiss, I would have from my sweet Jamie Boy. If I'd only known, I would have never let go.

I love you my sweet son, my sunshine, my Jamie Lou Who.

From Jamie's Community of Love

A llowing others to share their memories, thoughts, and feelings about the person you loved, and thought you knew completely, will shed light on and animate their life in new and different ways. This can bring you closer to knowing your loved one deeply in surprising, uplifting—sometimes even difficult—ways. It also allows those who are touched by (but not attached to) the loss to process their grief at *their* level, while also knowing that they have helped you on your long road of recovery.

When Jamie left his body, the stories poured in, and we encouraged them by having 3 x 5 cards at the memorial following the service, complete with a Sponge Bob (Jamie's favorite) cake and piñata for the kids. Having all these stories has helped me continue to see Jamie shining his light in the world which, in turn, allows me to savor and honor his life, however short.

When I first read these stories, I saw his legacy forming through the connections he had made across the generations. This validated my own belief that he had a heart full of love and joy, and that his "old soul" Spirit shined with inner wisdom and peace. In finding Jamie's legacy, I was able to keep moving forward and, hopefully, to help others going through such losses, including my family.

Here is a collection of stories and memories recounted by family, friends and acquaintances in the days, weeks and months after Jamie left his body about the mark he left on them:

◠•◡

"My prayers, thoughts and love continue to be with you. I haven't been by to visit for a while since I realized that my physical presence couldn't begin to mitigate your pain. But that doesn't mean that I think of you less, or miss either of you or Jamie any less. In fact, I still catch myself looking for Jamie in the child care when I get to church. The image of Jamie that really stands out to me is when we went hiking at Easter. What a great day that was and how beautiful Jamie was on the hike. He was so enthusiastic about hiking, and kept up with the adults. I think he went at least a couple of miles more than the adults, since he wanted to take every 'short cut' available (which were generally quite a bit longer than the trail). Then we went to breakfast and he was totally open to trying those blueberry things. I was so impressed the whole morning at his joy and enthusiasm for everything around him, with no fear of trying new foods, blazing a new path, checking out the trees on the trail, whatever.

The part that impressed me most about that morning was that he wanted to share his blueberry things with me. He really didn't know me that well, but was so certain to separate one for me before he even began eating. I was so impressed that such a little human had complete consideration of the people around him. I think he was even concerned that I not wait too long to eat it, in case it got cold. What beautiful, pure love for others.

Thanks so much bringing him into our lives. I continue to send out lots of love and prayers to you and all my hopes that you will find peace and joy again, despite the void that will never be filled. Jamie lived his life with peace and joy and wants nothing less for you, the people that taught him to love."
—Melanie G.

⌒•⌒

"Things About Jamie: As I sit down and try to remember my times with Jamie, I'm sad to say we didn't have a lot of time together. I would see him once or twice a year when he came to visit with his family. However, during those few hours a year that we spent together, he did make an impression on me. Here are a few of my fondest memories of him:

Jamie was gentle but rugged at the same time. I remember seeing him bow his head in prayer one minute then slide down the muddy hill by my condo the next. He was also very brave. He liked to watch shark attack movies with Lorenzo when he came to visit (I'm sure Elene didn't approve).

Jamie found pleasure in the little things. I remember one time while hiking in the Chino Hills State Park we were looking for wildlife. While we all scanned the hills looking for deer, coyotes, and mountain lions, he kept his eyes to the ground. We didn't spot much of anything; however, he was enthralled with the beetles and potato bugs that he kept us from stepping on.

I remember Jamie loved to eat. I saw him eat two bowls of oatmeal, a banana, a yogurt and a glass of juice in one sitting. Quite a feat for a 4-year-old! He was a dedicated vegetarian (although one time his cousin Demetri put

some bologna in his peanut butter sandwich). He could also mix a mean drink at Denny's (two parts water, one part creamer, a lemon wedge, a tomato slice, and two sugar packets. Mmmm!).

The last time Jamie and I were together, we talked about what he wanted to be when he grew up. He had it narrowed down to either dentist or bee-keeper. He was leaning towards beekeeper because he had recently discovered that many people have bad breath.

Later that same morning we arrived back at my condo to discover my dog Goldie had passed away while we were out for breakfast. I was surprised that he didn't ask a lot of questions about death like most children would have. He simply accepted death as a part of life and gently stroked her head. I think Jamie was very wise for his years. I feel lucky for the time I did have with Jamie. I will always remember him."

—**Jeff H.**

⌒•⌒

"I've just read all the writings about Jamie on your website. Thank you for sharing your love and your loss. When Denise broke the sad news to me, I felt disbelief and shock and could only imagine your loss. After reading these powerful poems and letters, I can now understand what you've lost. The ache in my own heart and the tears welling in my own eyes allow me a little insight to the enormity of your loss.

How has Jamie touched my life? Why was I, a stranger, included in his circle of light? Jamie, like a smooth pebble dropped into a calm lake, created rippling circles of ever-expanding connection. You and Elene were at the vortex, most deeply impacted, while I, even at the most outer ring, was still strongly influenced. Jamie has also touched my life in a subtle, yet most significant, way.

When I met Jamie at Tayo's baptismal luncheon, I was taking pictures of Adan holding Tayo with the San Diego skyline as the backdrop, the bright sun causing both of them to squint. Jamie was playing nearby, exploring the nooks and crannies of the rocks, shirtless in his black dress pants, the wind and sun making his mop of curls come alive. I invited him to pose with Adan and Tayo, a lively addition to Tayo's baptismal documentary. I immediately noticed how easy and carefree Jamie was, a natural free spirit, so comfortable in his surroundings. There was no self-consciousness or feelings of importance, just grace of movement. What caught my attention was his inner spark. Having become more discerning of people's facial expressions and personalities, seeing every nuance through the camera's viewfinder, I was struck by his honesty . . . in his eyes, in his movements, in his conversation, in his simple enjoyment of exploring his world in the most hands-on way. In my mind was an unspoken 'wow.'

Being a photographer, I felt the need to make that special portrait. I wanted to show Jamie's effortless charm. What a good sport he was, too. He enjoyed being in front of the camera . . . it was no big deal . . . he was just being himself. I put him next to some yellow daisies and he did the rest. I could have taken another dozen shots! It's not often that I get photogenic models who shine from within . . . it was a breeze. All I had to do was ask for a smile and press the shutter. Jamie was a rare photographic moment for me . . . a WOW.

So now, how has Jamie touched my life? By letting me know that Love with such depth really does exist. The love you have for Jamie is real. You've experienced it to the fullest and you're still experiencing the fullness of it, although this time, in the most painful way. I've yet to experience it. My own daughter is 25 years old now, my own miracle baby who came into this world at one pound, eight ounces . . . two months at the ICU, only four pounds, five ounces when brought home on Thanksgiving 1976. Yet, I've missed out on this deep loving, out of ignorance and lack of capacity. I don't know how such love feels . . . I could only imagine. I wish for it still . . .

Jamie had a lesson for me, a clue to unravel and piece together. Love and God lived in Jamie's heart. Life can be long or short, but without Love and God, life is just mere existence. How can I follow Jamie's example? How can I open up my own heart to more Love? Jamie at the age of five lived Love and God; and I, at 46, am still struggling.

Jamie was a special gift, a human angel with limited physical time, who so exuded Spirit that even strangers like me were blessed by his presence. Thank you, Jamie."
—**Merlin**

"Jamie was a very advanced thinker for his age group. I remember one Sunday when Miss JoAnn was asking her class if anyone remembered what their lesson was about during the previous week's Sunday school class. Jamie immediately raised his hand and explained the lesson to his friends. Then he went on to tie in that lesson with the theme for the current day's lesson! He was so knowledgeable in his Bible stories. He truly acknowledged the God within himself and in others. To be so young and yet so wise surely blesses us all in his brief touch with our own souls.

I will always remember you, little Jamie, and I will continue to acknowledge that wisdom you imparted to us all . . . God inside all of us, All of us one in God."
—**Rashna K.**

"Curly, naked, fearless Jamie! This is how I will always remember Jamie: When Carl and I lived in San Diego for the year before we got married, I

delighted in seeing Jamie on occasion when Elene and I worked on Family Group material for the Adults of Unity conference. Sometimes she and Jamie would come to my house, sometimes I would go to theirs.

One night in particular, I was on my way over from work, and it was COLD. As an east coast person, I had still not got it quite right with those San Diego nights. I never seemed to have a jacket in my car when I needed it. So, on the way over to their house, I made a quick stop home to pick up a sweater to keep in my car once and for all. I call it my 'San Diego sweater' even now. When I arrived, there was Jamie and his wild, beautiful curls dancing around naked. Elene explained with a simple shrug, 'He doesn't like to wear clothes.' He spent almost the entire evening naked, naked in the most unselfconscious way: watching TV, eating dinner, pushing his trucks on the floor, doing all the usual things a little boy does, just—naked. Meanwhile, I was eyeing the room; surely, they have a fireplace in here, right?

Later that night, when it was almost his bedtime, Jamie wanted me to see his room. He had these great bunk beds, and he promptly climbed to the top bunk and, without warning, flung himself down into my arms. So fearless and trusting, it never crossed his mind that I could miss.

Jesus said we need to be like little children. I think being like Jamie is exactly what he meant: unselfconscious, full of life, fearless and trusting that we will be taken care of. And not letting it cross our minds that it could be otherwise. I love you all and wish I could be with you. Elene, Mychael and Danielle, I know God will take care of you, it couldn't be otherwise."
—Carol, Carl and Angela C.

❧

"Dear Jamie: This morning I had another memory. A year ago, when Jerry, Demetri and I were packing our belongings and preparing to move out of your

house, you came to me and asked, 'Why are you leaving, Auntie?' I explained to you, to the best of my ability, that this is what mommies and daddies do when they get married and start their lives together. I also explained that it was getting too crowded for us in your house and that we needed our own space. Your response moved me to tears then and still does now. I just wish I  *had been wise enough to reciprocate at the time. You said, 'I'm gonna miss you guys when you go,' and, 'I'll be sad when you leave.' Now, I'm the one missing you and the one who is sad. I only hope that you left this earth knowing that I thought of you as one of my own. I love you Jamie. I always will."*
—**Auntie**

"Most parents think their child is special, so when I heard Mychael and Elene talk about Jamie, I listened—because it's natural for parents to brag. However, in the case of Jamie, a mutual friend, Marcia, also talked about how special he was. Since they lived in San Diego and I in Missouri, I thought it was unlikely that I would ever know for myself who this special child of God was. But God had a plan, which meant I was to come out to San Diego for work business.

As I made plans to come to San Diego, there was an urging in my soul to see Elene and of course to meet Jamie, so we made plans to see each other. I will never forget the day I met Jamie. He was such a beautiful child with a head full of curls, a very warm and gracious little host, who greeted me with a big smile and a snuggling kind of hug. He asked me questions about myself and my sons. We ate together, sharing our food. Our time together eventually evolved into a conversation about God and about his remembrances of time before he came into this life experience. I was in awe of this precious soul.

Jamie talked about the beauty of the world, we as adults sometimes forget. We gave each other our full attention—our souls meshed. Jamie talked about how he loved God and how God loved him. But most impressive was our dialogue about angels. He told me how they were everywhere and how they surrounded him and how we need angels to help us. He pointed out that he could see angels surrounding me. There was a joyous communion between our souls and our Creator.

My visit was not with Mychael and Elene. It was with Jamie. I left their home feeling as though I had been with an ancient master teacher, who knew and enjoyed his oneness with God—a happy soul that exuded an untarnished pureness of God's love. A perfect expression of the beauty of spirit at work through a young human body. Jamie, a masterpiece of beauty and love in its purest form. A masterpiece that continues to walk in eternal love with God and the angels that he loved so dearly."

—Pat Anderson Williams, Adults of Unity Coordinator, Association of Unity Churches

"The Blessing of Jamie: Ever since I began teaching Jamie in the general class at the age of three, he lit up the classroom. He was so bright, so charming, had such a light about him, and was a friend to everyone. When he came into my 3–5-year-old class, I became amazed at the wisdom he had for his age. He always knew the answers. Just back last Palm Sunday, I was teaching about Jesus riding the donkey into Jerusalem, and I asked why the donkey likes Jesus. Jamie said, 'Because Jesus was kind to him and gave him good things to eat.' And then Jamie said, 'This was the same donkey Mary rode into Bethlehem.'

When I said only common people rode donkeys, Jamie immediately chimed in and said, 'That's because Jesus was the king of God's world, not of this world.' The lesson had told me to make this point. I was supposed to make this point with the children but Jamie was ahead of me! When we did the lesson on Jesus blessing the children, Jamie said, 'Jesus said "the kingdom of heaven was for those like the children" because the children like him loved Jesus the best.' Jamie had such a sweet, loving nature.

He would never fight or call names; if he accidentally hit or pushed someone, he was always ready to apologize. All the children in my class got along well with him. At the last birthday party, he was so proud he would be turning six and moving up (to the next Sunday school class). He was always so excited about attending class and would march over singing loudly, 'I am walking in the light,' even when I didn't start it. When I started the prize box each month for perfect attendance, he made sure he came every week, and was always so excited to pick his prize. He could barely decide because everything interested him.

He radiated vibrant health and life. But in spite of all his deep inner wisdom, he was very much a regular little boy who enjoyed the typical things a 5-year-old boy does—it just seemed with much greater intensity. When he got his jacket with the detachable sleeves, all during play time he wanted to throw them high in the air and catch them. When we had balloons for the birthday parties, he played volleyball with them. He was so proud that he could go across the jungle gym with his feet almost touching the ground, and how many cookies he could eat at snack time.

He loved to dress up, and when we acted out the nativity play in class, he insisted on being the 'Black King.' Co-Co the bear, the puppet I use in class, was Jamie's special friend. Jamie didn't see him as a puppet, but as a real bear, and would grab him and give him a hug after hug. One Sunday when we were all telling each other things that we loved, and Co-Co said he loved honey and having his back scratched, Jamie said, 'I'll scratch your back for you Co-Co,' and reached over and did it. That was Jamie all over—Love in Action.

I called my brother Ray in New York to tell him Jamie had been killed and that I was grieving. Ray had visited my class once, but he immediately said, 'I remember Jamie!' He said, 'Jamie was so lively and bright and intel-

ligent, he just stood out.' I have grieved terribly in losing Jamie, but in one way it has been a blessing to me, so Jamie is still doing good for others. It made me realize how precious all my little ones are to me, and how much I love them, since I never got to have children of my own, how they have blessed me—especially Jamie."

—Laura

~·~

"I met Jamie one time in his short life, and it was about six weeks before his death. I had attended a workshop at Christ Church Unity, and was saying goodbye to people near the parking lot. I saw Jamie playing with a friend and, without thinking, spontaneously approached them and initiated a game in which I stood on a stoop and pretended to be giving a serious speech about a very important topic. Then, right in the middle of a sentence, I would 'invol-untarily' fall (jump) off the stoop, jumbling the sentence into gibberish as I fell. Jamie laughed uproariously, and proceeded to get on the stoop and engage in his own 'serious' speech, followed by the clumsy fall.

Giggles abounded as Jamie, his friend and myself took turns giving speeches and 'falling' off the stoop. I was touched and struck by how easily and quickly Jamie let me, an adult stranger, into his world, as well as how he instantly understood the spirit and the humor of what I had playfully created. Mychael and Elene told me later that Jamie adopted the game and made it his own, giving speeches all through that week and beyond.

I left the parking lot with a glow of satisfaction, having made a connection with a very bright, joyous soul. I'm so glad I had a chance to meet him before his passing, though [our meeting] was brief."

—Scott K.

⌒·⌒

"I liked when Jamie and me (Adam) played Megaman and with his Legos. Jamie was real fun and very animated."

—Adam, neighborhood and school friend

⌒·⌒

"Jamie always had a lot of energy, a smile and shared his love in Sunday school! He sang loudly and loved to pray. We miss him and love him."

—Jacquie

⌒·⌒

"I first met Jamie when I taught in the nursery. I knew he was special then. Jamie and I bonded because we share the knowledge of Spanish. He was so eager and full of life. Along the years I would see him running around the church grounds, so full of life. He was and is a special child. We will all miss him."

—Melva

⌒•⌒

"I will remember the joy and enthusiasm he expressed. I will remember how lovingly Jamie washed your feet, Elene, at the foot washing service this past Easter week. He was singing and smiling and washing. My partner and I sat next to both of you. It was beautiful. I remember his energy in Sunday school. He was my teacher. I'll never forget his smiling eyes, beautiful hair and the way music called him. There was no chance of him not dancing or playing the guitar, air style, when he heard music. He added joy to our lives. God's peace."
—Patti S.

⌒•⌒

"I love you Jamie opt (but) *I wish you were stis* (still) *alive. I miss you a lot."*
—Lyric, Jamie's six-year-old cousin and friend

"I loved watching the love Elene expressed as she videotaped Jamie up on the stage at CCU. I shared with you, Elene, that I didn't know who I enjoyed watching more—you or sweet Jamie. His light shines on. Blessings."
—Kathy S.

"I have many memories of Jamie: Asking for candy on Sundays; peering over Nathan's shoulder giggling; his enthusiasm singing out in the children's Christmas program; in his little tux on the day of the wedding, saying, 'Mom, your dress looks like a tent!' and his beautiful smile and love of life."
—Meredith T.

"Everyone loved Jamie. That head of curls, engaging smile, love of life, love of play, lots of laughter and joy to all he came in contact with. Nurtured by love, Jamie was love.

I first noticed him hiding underneath all those curls. He was beautiful. He was holding Elene's hand and hiding behind her legs. He was very quiet, so I missed the chance to talk with him. He took a seat next to you and soon went to sleep. I will never forget how beautiful he looked on that day, dressed in a little suit. After he woke up, I got a chance to see him bounce to your car. He was beautiful. He was a gift and I wish I would have been lucky enough to be loved by Jamie.

Elene, Mychael and Jamie came to the house for dinner and to discuss business details of an Adults of Unity conference we were a part of planning. After dinner Karl, Mychael and Elene began their meeting. I decided to hang out with Jamie and be filled in on the details later. I showed Jamie the toy selection I had. He sifted through things and found a kaleidoscope! He eagerly explored it and looked through it like a pirate seeking land. He was instantly taken by all the colors and shapes he saw and carried on lengthy conversations with the kaleidoscope practically glued to his eye.

Together we discovered that if you put objects in front of the kaleidoscope, the pattern and colors change. Jamie got so excited about what he was now calling 'the movie' that he HAD to show his parents and Karl! He quickly made it to the office in a variety of runs, jumps and skips! He excitedly entered and stated that he had something to show them, 'a movie!' Elene and Mychael have a natural ease in their ability to prioritize a situation when it comes to parenting, and both in unison stopped what they were doing.

After everyone rejoiced with Jamie, we left, to let them finish up the meeting. Jamie was obviously very pleased by the shared excitement for his discovery, as he grinned from ear to ear. He turned to me and gleefully said, 'We are so LUCKY!' 'Why?' I asked. 'Because we get to play and the adults . . . have to do all the boring stuff.' 'Oh,' I chuckled. 'Yeah, they sit around and just talk, that is boring!'

In that moment, Jamie believed he was the luckiest boy in the world. Not only had he discovered the magic of the kaleidoscope, he also rescued his parents and Karl from adulthood!

My experience of spending time with Jamie is continually having my heart explode with love and wonder. After a few hours, I said to Mychael, 'How do you live with your heart exploding every 30 seconds with love? Is that what it's like for you?' Mychael responded, 'All the time and it's great!'

I remember Jamie as all boy! His way was the experiential way! He always seemed to believe he could do anything. He curled 8-pound weights at age 5 with a huge smile on his face and leapt off any step or platform. I remember one time he was lifting himself up with his arms onto the kitchen counter.

Elene gently said, 'Be careful.' 'I CAN DO IT!' he boldly argued. Well, he certainly was strong, making his way halfway up, but wasn't quite strong enough. He slipped, bumping his chin. Jamie was more startled than hurt. All checked in on his wellbeing. Not one 'I told you so' comment was made. Jamie merely seemed to learn that it didn't work that time, and from the look in his eyes you knew he would try again."

—Jeanne L.

A Collection of Love Notes: Written while Jamie was in Ms. Debbie's class between two-and-a-half to three years old:

"Jamie is Mr. Sport! He loves playing basketball, baseball. Soccer. He even cheers on his friends. I love it when he says, 'Hold Me' with the sweetest smile. Then he grabs my hair. He is such a lovey boy."

"Jamie is good at calling our friendly squirrels to come and eat. He gets so excited when they come running up the hill. I'm so proud of him."

"Jamie is so mature and very huggy. He had a fantastic time in his new environment and is making lots of friends. He kept saying, 'My baby friends' while giving hugs. Too cute! Jamie loves to paint. We painted huge cardboard boxes outside to make a choo-choo train."

"Jamie loves bugs. He collects ants, roly pollies, caterpillars and worms. He picks them up with a shovel and puts them gently into a bucket. He is always so proud of his collection."

"Jamie loves dairy products. He enjoyed tasting all the different cheeses. His favorite was colorful yogurt. Jamie is such a sweetheart. He hugs every parent that walks through the door."

"Jamie is a snuggly bear. He gives out the warmest full body hugs. I love it! Especially when he twirls my hair and hums a lullaby-bye. Too precious!! Jamie has a very positive heart."

"Thank you, for being so supportive and always lending a helping hand."

"Jamie is such a busy boy. He happily gets involved in every activity. Jamie loves to get messy—and he is proud of his mess he creates. Especially if it is an art activity. Jamie is having a great time."

"Jamie is such a great boy. He is very easygoing but a leader at the same time. In the short time that he has been here, he has become everyone's favorite playmate."

A collection of stories from our next-door neighbor, and Jamie's good friend, Patti G.:

"I held Jamie when he was home—day one or two of his beginning. Slightly fussy, Mychael explained Jamie was awaiting 'food' and Elene was in the bathroom. I just swayed with the sweet baby in my arms, who forgot about eating and went soundly to sleep."

"We had frogs on our welcome mat. Jamie used to come over and do 'frog jumping' and 'ribbets' all over the porch and up and down the sidewalk."

"Jamie loved to come over and play at Patti's. Once we had a sword fight with his plastic sword and my pen. We played and laughed and even chased him up the street (to capture the pirate)."

"Jamie loved to come over and ask for candy or feed the little gold fish in the table-top aquarium. He always had questions about everything. 'Why can't the fish come out of there?' He loved to wind the music box and play with the view master."

"Last summer, hearing hysterical laughter from the front yard, I looked over to find Demetri doubled over in laughter while a naked Jamie was nonchalantly 'hands free' peeing in the front yard."

"When Jamie came home from the hospital after breaking his arm, I brought him some candy, watermelon flavored ('It's good for you because it has water in it,' according to Jamie), and a very tiny bear. He told me he was naming it 'Lovey.' The next day he was giving it rides in his sling."

"I will always remember seeing his curly head and barely seeing his eyes as Mychael backed into the driveway. He always looked to see what was going on! He even had me eat a flower one day (making sure I ate it all) that his dad said was okay to eat."

"A few months ago, Jamie came over very early and was going to have break-fast, get dressed, etc. and go to the bus stop. On our porch I explained that we had to be very quiet, as no one else was up yet. Walking into the kitchen and seeing the coffee maker brewing (loudly), Jamie proclaimed: 'That's loud.'"

"We missed the sailing of the Star of India, so we went to maybe see it at the point. We were right in the middle of the clouds rolling by, and he got to climb a tree, see the view, touch the old armor, see where San Diego is on a California map and hold a real sword. WOW!! Jamie was dressed for the occasion in his pirate outfit."

"Super Hero Jamie. Running around our yard, over at our house, etc. With his cape on—sometimes with clothes; lots of times—cape only!! Happy and Free."

"My favorite memory is when Gary and I took Jamie and Demetri to the Zoo. It was Jamie's fourth birthday. We went on the zoo bus ride. Very loudly at each stop, Jamie would ask: 'What is it?' 'What does it do?' 'Where does it live?' 'Does it have a tail?' When viewing any nature show, we still ask each other, 'Does it have a tail?' It was a wonderful, fun-filled adventure!"

"Recently, watching Gary using a shovel in our yard, Jamie (thinking of a rototiller?) stated, 'That's how they did it in the old days.' He also 'helped' drag a chunk of concrete and a post, telling Gary, 'You couldn't have done it without a little help.'"

"Last time I saw Jamie, he had made finger marks across the mud in our yard. He was gleefully stomping through the compost pile. Asking him what would Mom and Dad say if he came home with muddy feet, he replied, 'They'll probably give me a time out.' (Well worth it.)"

❧

Notes From Our Azalea Park Neighbors:

"Jamie, I remember you sitting across the road waiting for the school bus. Whoever was with you, your friend of the family was flapping because they thought the bus had already left. You just looked so relaxed taking it all in stride. I also remember you coming into our garage and finding the dress up box. The armor of God was your favorite. We will miss you."
—Kurt, Melanie, Kyle & Lauren

"I want to let you know that you and Jamie are in my thoughts and prayers. You are wonderful neighbors and we love you. I can't think of one particular story of Jamie but I want to share with you my thoughts. Every time I go in the front yard, I see Jamie climbing your tree. Every time I go on our deck, I see Jamie playing in the back yard. I can hear his voice in my head. I had a dream a few nights ago that I was swinging Jamie in a circle and we were spinning. He crawled into my arms and we were hugging and spinning. When I woke up, I could still feel him. I Love You."
—Rebecca

"Have you ever had someone in your life that likes everything that you like? Have you ever had someone in your life that wanted to be like you in every way? Have you ever been a role model for someone special? For me, that some-one was Jamie!

Jamie was the coolest little five year old I knew. We liked and did the same things. We watched Sponge Bob together. We played knights and dragons because I was his role model.

Even though I was Jamie's role model, we looked nothing alike. I had

short, straight black hair, brown eyes
and dark skin. Jamie, on the other
hand, had long, curly hair that
changed color from brown to blonde.
He had green eyes and peach skin.
Even though we looked nothing alike
and we were only cousins, we called
each other brothers. He was my little Jamie.

 Unfortunately for me and my whole family, my little Jamie was taken
from me. There was a car accident involving my mom's little Toyota and a
huge truck. My mom was in the hospital for a couple months. Jamie never
made it. Jamie will always be in my heart."

—Demetri, 11 years old. Cousins by blood, brothers by love.

Heaven Is No Different From Jamie. "Jamie Is Alright."

I dreamt that I was in heaven and I saw my whole family. Including grand-
mas and grandpas I have never seen, also other family members. Then I saw

my mom, Aunt Elene, and my Aunt
Angela. It seemed they were smiling
the whole time, then they guided me
to Jamie. I saw Jamie and he told
God all the phrases that he made up
about God. God looked at him and
laughed. After that I felt like every-
thing was okay. After that it felt like
I fell back to Earth safely asleep in my

bed. Then I woke up from my dream and ran to my mom's bedroom and told her about my dream. Then after I said to my mom, 'Mom, trust me when I say this, Jamie is alright.' My mom said, 'Honey, I know, we all know.'"
—**Alexis (Jamie's cousin)**

⌁

The following story is printed in Loving Memory of Lynne McNeeley, Jamie's grandma. Ma, you are so loved and so missed. It is my great wish that you and Jamie are playing together and getting to know each other.

"The Healing Circle"

A couple weeks after I was diagnosed with cancer, friends wanted to have a hands on healing circle for me. I am a deep believer in prayer and of course "hands on" since I do Healing. The morning of my healing circle, I said my prayers and tried to figure out how one prepared for the event that was going to be held in my honor. I had been wondering that for some time and simply didn't know how to express the appreciation and pressure. I prayed that I could remain, or become open enough to receive, the blessings that were offered. As we all gathered, prayers were offered up—the first of many prayers that special morning. Everyone added something and we closed knowing that our prayers were already answered. I felt more ready to meet the rest of the morning's happenings but still a little nervous. As I began to relax, there was a moment when I could feel the entire group settle down and become one. From that point on I felt in an altered state—relaxed but very intense. I could feel the work that was being done on my behalf, yet I was still so intensely involved in what was happening inside me. When I relaxed some, I said, "I wonder if Lazarus was tired after he rose from the dead?" There were giggles in the circle.

At that point I saw Jamie. It was just his little face smiling at me. I thought he was there because Kathryn had mentioned him, so I called for my grandmother in a test to see if I was just imagining Jamie's presence. She did not appear and his little face ringed with curls just kept smiling at me. I said out loud, "Jamie is here." I then started crying from the deepest part of me. I sobbed like I have never sobbed in the presence of others. Finally, I settled down and I could see Jamie had moved and was now sitting on a rock and he was speaking to me. I couldn't hear him but I knew he was speaking to me. His lips were not moving. And then I heard, not Jamie's voice, or even in an auditory way, "Daddy's here." He said that several times. I repeated that out loud and said, "I don't know what that means." Then he was gone.

Things settled into a quietness for a few minutes and I could feel it was complete.

—July 19, 2003 by Jamie's *Aunie* (Grandma)

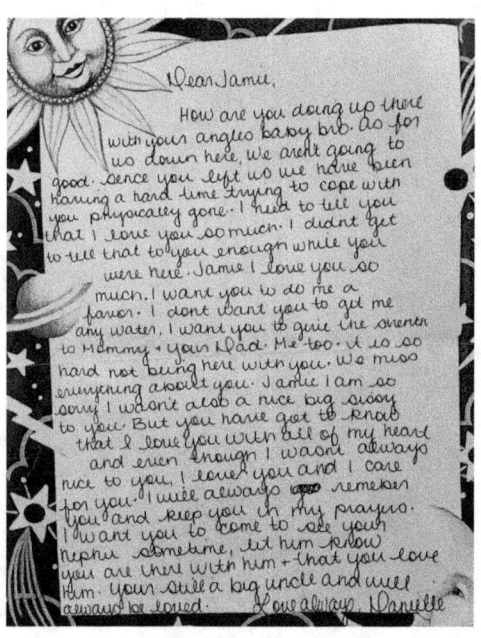

Jamie

Mi mamá me
canta angelito.

CHAPTER FOURTEEN

Preserving Memories
Identifying Your Loved One's Legacy

———

I t is easy to be scattered and forgetful when grieving, so having a conscious plan to collect and preserve memories can be helpful. I have found that it is a tendency to learn a lot more about a person after they have passed. Sometimes even painful facts can be discovered, revealed, or talked about after a person passes. This can be true even when that someone is young if they have friends outside of your purview, such as at school, with other family members, etc. (Even with Jamie—I learned that certain family members were sneaking lunch meat into his PB&J sandwiches!)

Capturing Memories—Developing a Legacy

There are many options for collecting memories from others, but if you have the opportunity to talk to your loved one while they are still here, to capture their essence, this can be very comforting after their passing. Use video or audio to record stories directly from a person as a matter of routine, knowing that we will all pass through that door at some point, regardless of whether that passing is imminent or not.

Once you are at the point of being at a wake or during a visit with people that knew your loved one, have your video or audio device(s) ready to record the stories of willing individuals.

Place 3 x 5 cards on the tables at the repass or during visits for written memories and stories. Include a question sheet of things you would like to know.

Upload your pictures and video on a social platform such as Facebook, or create a website. This duplication will ensure they will be preserved.

Hang pictures wherever you want in your space, for as long as you want.

Journal your story of the relationship. There are workbooks you can purchase that can help you capture memories, such as "Fire in My Heart, Ice in My Veins" or "Storybook," for example.

Make a list of your loved one's "favorites." We become so afraid we would forget stuff, and sometimes, over time, we do. This can help us feel safer and confident that we won't forget the intimate details of our loved ones' lives over time.

Make a list of little quirks or sayings, and if you have these recorded in their voice that makes it even more meaningful.

Plant a tree, put in a bench, name a street, create a park. I know some of this may sound out of reach, but Jamie was able to inspire all of these things, and with neighbors' support, we did all of these in the very community we lived.

If you have the interest, start a non-profit or memorial fund, scholarship or other form of community involvement that carries on the legacy or memory of your loved one. Most major communities have foundations where these legacies can be started without a lot of work by the bereaved. They usually have a minimum donation to start up. An example of this where I live is The San Diego Foundation.

What Does It Mean to Leave a Legacy?

The term *legacy* normally means that the person has affected change on the world in a positive way. People who are successful at something can leave a legacy of positive change in that area.

But everyone leaves a legacy, no matter if they lived for what seems like a short time and didn't appear to have a body of work, personal interests, passions, a life's mission, or a personality that spoke to their legacy. Sometimes legacies are found in their death by preventing others from experiencing a similar loss. Sometimes the legacy will come to you in a time of reflection, a deep knowing or even in a dream. Other times you will need to think about your loved one and consider what their legacy can be. Below are some things to ponder in connecting to your loved one's legacy.

The number one way to keep your loved one's legacy alive is to talk about them.

Don't be afraid to say their name and include them in the family. When the loss is fresh you might still set a place at the table, hold a chair at events, or wear their clothes. You may pass their clothes on to others to wear, make a quilt from their clothing and display it, celebrate their birthday, introduce them to the next generation, make it okay to bring them up, to talk about them, to continue to cry and show love toward them. The more you do so, the more others will be comfortable to do so alongside you, and with their own losses. In this way, our lost loves won't feel so far away or forgotten, especially as time keeps slipping into the future.

Ask Questions to Focus the Legacy

Did my loved one have a passion? (The outdoors, animal rights, civil rights, Second Amendment rights, art, plays, museums, politics, religion, parks, social justice, sports, pets, etc.)

Did my loved one have a body of work that they took pride in that they would want continued or carried on? (Working for a medical cure, studying an ancient language, preserving the planet, teaching yoga, etc.)

Did my loved one pass from something "avoidable" that I want to make a difference in their name for, such as gun violence, suicide, cancer, rare genetic condition, drowning, allergy, overdose?

What attributes did my loved one have that I want to honor? Did they exude care toward others, have a hilarious sense of humor? Were they an "endearing curmudgeon," a bright light, a compassionate soul?

Sometimes it's the loved one's *characteristics* that define their legacy, such as in Jamie's case. Because he was young, he didn't yet have a career or passion. But even so, his humanness made his legacy clear: Love*Joy*Peace*Connection. And, because his life was taken through a car crash caused by distracted driving, that also became a focus, by giving a face to the high price of "driving under the influence" of the cell phone. We stumbled onto a third facet of Jamie's legacy through our own experience of grieving our loss, in that we felt we had to help our friends learn how to support us in our grief. It became part of the work of Jamie's legacy to provide grief support and literacy.

So, over time, our young son Jamie's legacy was shown to have four distinct branches: 1. His humanness we could share and exude with others forever as "Love*Joy*Peace*Connection." 2. Being the face of the dangers of distracted driving in an effort to save future lives from this type of loss.

3. Providing grief support and literacy to others and our society. 4. Living our lives to the fullest. Living our lives out loud.

We could not have guessed that would be the case,
and it is a beautiful thing that endures.

Jamie's joy was clear, which helped us find Jamie's legacy quickly, but it isn't always that clear, so take your time. It will come as you maintain your connection and love for your person. Their continued presence will guide you and you will absolutely know when you have it.

Our Moms and Dads
are kind of like
our spirit self, for
helping the kids and
for rubbing their
backs
—Jamie

Para
Papá

CHAPTER FIFTEEN

Strategies for Coping, Grieving & Healing

What You Need To Know

- Always listen to yourself, your body knows what to do.
- Don't try to outrun your grief. No amount of alcohol, drugs, food, sex, work, etc. will make it better. *You must be willing to feel it and process the experience.*
- Tell others what you need.
- Find out about the process you are in.
- Be gentle with your feelings and thought processes.
- Avoid self-judgment.
- Do not put "should have" on yourself.

- Find a supportive person or people you can trust. Be vulnerable to share your pain and humble enough to accept support.
- Give yourself time for healing. Grief cannot be rushed. It is a slow, sure, unpredictable process.
- Know that the overwhelming feelings you have now will soften as you learn to live beside them.
- Avoid unrealistic expectations or goals of yourself or those that others put on you. Learn to say "NO!" (I.e. Drive yourself in case you feel the need to leave "NOW," or have an "escape hatch" should you no longer want to be someplace or feel the need to hide for a moment. An example of this: Jamie's dad had a closet at work he could escape to when he got overwhelmed on the job.)
- Be aware of your body's need for good nutrition, gentle or vigorous exercise, fresh air, perhaps massage, and massive doses of rest and relaxation.
- Surround yourself with life, plants, animals, friends, special music, etc.
- Release tension, anger, sorrow and frustration by: crying alone or with someone; writing anything—poetry, stories, essays, a letter to your loved one, yourself, the Universe or God; taking a walk or a nap; drawing how you feel; making a scrapbook of photos or memorabilia, keeping a journal or diary, etc.
- Maintain as "regular" a schedule as possible.
- Forgive yourself and others.
- Prepare for change, new interests, new friends, solitude, and growth.
- Remember: Grief is a spiral of feelings, thoughts, seasons and experiences. It is not a straight line with a beginning and ending point. The process of grief is healing the pain of loss and keeping the treasured memories and love within your heart. It is learning to live in the present pain with hope for the future.

What the Bereaved Want Others to Know

This was the manifesto we posted on our front door in the earliest stages of our grief. Feel free to replace all references to "he/him," which we use to reference our son, Jamie, with whichever pronoun is appropriate for your lost loved one: he/she/they/him/her/them.

- PLEASE, don't expect us to get over it. We will never be quite the same people and we'll never be over losing our loved one.
- PLEASE, don't tell us he's "in a better place." He's not here with us.
- PLEASE, don't tell us you understand, or know how we feel, unless you've lost a child. And even then, every loss is different, and you can't possibly know how someone else feels exactly, so ask instead of telling, just listen and support each other on your own paths.
- PLEASE, don't expect us to feel better. Bereavement is not a condition that clears up.
- PLEASE, don't ask us, "How are you?" It is part of a greeting that, at this time, makes no sense to us and can't be answered with a simple "fine."
- PLEASE, don't tell us "it was meant to be," or he's in heaven, or an angel, always with you, etc. . . . He was *our* meant to be, *our* heaven, *our* angel and he was with us in our home, and we will always miss him in his body. Whatever other conclusions we come to, we must do so on our own. Your absolute beliefs about the uncertain do not comfort us at this time.
- PLEASE, don't tell us that we are strong or that God never gives us more than we can bear. We would gladly be weak people if it would bring back our loved one.
- PLEASE, simply ask if there is anything you can do. It's hard for us to think, but we do need things. Even coming by to help with the most mundane task eases our burden. Offer some food, take us on a walk,

clean the bathroom, pick up something at the store. These tasks get lost in our constant grieving and are hard to ask for.

- PLEASE, just say you feel for us, you're sorry for our loss.
- PLEASE, just share your memories of our child with us. Say his name.
- PLEASE, just let us talk about our pain.
- PLEASE, listen to yourself; if you don't know what to say, just be with us in silence.
- PLEASE, just let us talk about our son.
- PLEASE, just keep coming around us, even though it's hard. Don't give up on us.
- PLEASE, just let us cry. Let us cry out, again and again. Our pain is based on real loss that hurts for a lifetime.
- PLEASE, just grieve with us.

PLEASE, PLEASE, PLEASE:
- Let us feel grief for as long as it takes.
- Listen and allow yourself to be moved.
- Show us you can stand beside us in the depth of our loss.
- Bear the deep silence with us.
- Open your arms. Hold us until we can breathe again.
- Encourage us to discover what helps us heal and ease the pain.
- Validate our pain and our right to feel it even if you don't understand.
- Be real with us. Don't just say religious slogans, dogma or advice that makes *you* more comfortable. Ask us what comforts us.
- You're right, we are *not* the same. Don't judge us. Allow us time to discover who we are in the wake of our loss.
- Be patient with our process.

UNTIL

Until we are both together again

Both on the same plane

My constant prayer will be
that you will experience this
earth in my body and that I will
experience heaven in your spirit

In this way we are always
together

As One

Inspired during the silence. Unity Village, MO Adults of Unity
© 2003 Elene Bratton

To Honor You

To honor you, I get up every day and take a breath. And start another day
without you in it.

To honor you, I laugh and love with those who knew your smile And, the way
your eyes twinkled with mischief and secret knowledge.

To honor you, I take the time to appreciate everyone I love, I know now there is
no guarantee of days or hours spent in their presence.

To honor you, I listen to music you would have liked and, sing at the top of my
lungs, with the windows rolled down.

To honor you, I take chances, say what I feel, hold nothing back, Risk making a
fool of myself, dance every dance.

You were my light, my heart, my gift of love, from the very highest source. So,
every day, I vow to make a difference, share a smile, live, laugh and love.
Now I live for us both, so all I do, I do to honor you.

Written By Connie F. Kiefer Byrd in Loving Memory of Jordan Alexander Kiefer 8/24/88 – 12/13/05

Greif vs. Depression - Some Differences

Grief	Depression
Loss is identifiable	Loss may or may not be identifiable
The focus is on the loss	Your focus is on yourself
Fluctuation in the ability to feel pleasure	Inability to feel pleasure
Variable physical symptoms	Chronic physical problems
Shutting down others is usually temporary	Persistent isolation
Fluctuating emotions	Fixed emotions, "feeling stuck"
Feelings of sadness and emptiness	Feeling of no hope and chronic emptiness
Relatively stable self-esteem	Loss of self-esteem, feeling like you're worthless
Some specific guilt/remorse	Generally, a global sense of guilt
Thoughts of wanting to be with the deceased not a current desire to die	Thoughts of suicide, usually as a result of wanting to stop the pain and not look at other options
Extra-sensory experiences (e.g. feeling the presence of the deceased)	Hallucinations and/or psychosis

Many people equate grief with depression, and it can even be diagnosed after one year of bereavement. But grief is not a disorder. It is a normal, and common, human reaction to loss. The bigger the loss, the bigger and longer the grief. Don't judge yourself: Instead, embrace yourself, embrace your process. Your grief is as big as your love and, oftentimes, lasts forever. But it does soften. I liken it to my sobriety: No one would judge me because I still seek support with over 30 years sober. So don't let anyone judge the length of your grief journey. Don't block it. Find the supports you need and keep learning to live beside it.

Jamie announced: "I have a girlfriend."
I asked him "What's her name?" he replies "I don't know."

—Jamie

CHAPTER SIXTEEN

Healing Through
Poems & Writings

Writing came to me like a savior from the recesses of my heart and mind. It came organically and naturally from a depth of my soul, from a spiritual place that could only be forged out of this specific pain. Much of it was affectionately named "the ramblings of a crazed, bereaved mom" as I spilled my heart out into multiple tape recordings made over years. Some of it I really liked. It helped me process my emotions and the trauma that comprises the sea of grief.

Sharing poems and essays, even those of others that I've curated, below and throughout this book, is not just to express ideas but also to encourage the bereaved to explore alternative healing practices. Poetry may not be your "thing," and you may not consider yourself a "right brain/artistic type." But I encourage you to at least try a free-form practice—be it paint-ing, doodling, Zen-tangle, mandalas, playing an instrument, drawing, dancing, yoga—and whatever else I may not even be aware of. Be open to finding a process, a practice, a way to express—in order to provide you with a break, a moment of solace. A feeling of peace. It won't save you from the lifelong journey, but it may offer some respite along the way.

Below are some of my more promising offerings for your consider-ation. (You will see the "substitute your loved one's name here" prompts on occasion. Feel free to do so with any of these.)

Three Prayers of Grief by Jamie's Mom, Elene Bratton

AM Prayer of Grief

Dear Mother and Father of the Universe,
Who know the suffering and love of the world through the eyes of parents
Who know the suffering of the loss of a child
And all those that leave their bodies too soon
Leaving their loved ones behind on this earth not knowing what to do
Not understanding why
Suffering a great sense of loss and devastation,
Let your presence and essence be with us today

Help us to know someone understands our pain and has compassion for
    our experience and insight into all that we endure each day in our sorrow.

Great Mother of Compassion
Great Father of Strength

Bless us today

Bless us as we try again on this earth

Bless our sorrow

Comfort our pain

Strengthen our resolve to continue for another day in the land of great grief

Father Universe

Help us find some humor in this day

Carry us on your shoulders

Mother Universe

Soothe our sadness

Hold us in your bosom

Bless us, Father and Mother Universe,

Who have known pain throughout the history of time

Who have experienced the anguish of losing so many, too soon

And who have developed great compassion for the sorrow of those who no
    longer have their loved ones

And for the loved ones themselves

Wherever they may be,

Help them in whatever ways they need, and,

Assist them to make the transition

Into peace

Father and Mother Universe

Hold us individually and together in your love and compassion today.

Evening Prayer of Grief

Dear Mother and Father of the Universe

Who know the suffering and love of the world through the heart of a parent

Who know the suffering of the loss of a child

And all those that leave their bodies too soon

Let your presence and essence be with us tonight

Great Mother of Compassion

Great Father of Strength

Help us this night to find a deep rest and comfort in sleep

Bless us with a vision or dream of our lost love

And for the loved ones themselves

Wherever they may be

Help them in whatever ways they need, and,

Help them to make the transition

Into peace

Father and Mother Universe

Hold us individually and together in your love and compassion this night.

Prayer for the Loved One

Dear Mother and Father of the Universe

Help our loved one* who has left their body

Comfort them in the light of Love

Their experience is unknown to us now

But our love is forever true

Let them know of our love and hear our heart's desire, even through our
   anguished tears,

That although our senses limit our contact, we wish to be with them every day,

That our arms ache to hold them

This is our earthly experience

And although it is very real

We do not want it to hinder them from doing what their path now calls

Make them know we wish them all good

Mother Universe

Wrap our loved one in your arms now

Let them feel the same love we shared here on earth

Father Universe

Give our loved one your gentle strength

Play with them until they are overjoyed with laughter

Father and Mother Universe

Hold us individually and together in your love and compassion until

we are reunited and throughout eternity.

*Can replace the generic "they" with their name or preferred pronouns

To Tie or Not to Tie

I see

the light in the darkness

the hope in the despair

love in the hatred,

faith in the questions

healing in the pain

life in the emptiness

We untie ourselves from the struggles that set us free and

give ourselves entirely to the hope of love.

Jamie's life brought me the most joy a person can ever know

Jamie's death brought me the most pain a person can ever know

That is why I also see

there is darkness in the light

despair in the hope

hatred in the love,

questions in the faith

pain in the healing

emptiness in the life

That is why we must tie ourselves to the struggle and bind ourselves

entirely to the possibility that there is no hope at all.

© Elene Bratton 8/15/2018

So Holy is Your Presence

Jamie

So Holy is your presence in my heart.

I honor your life within my own

Spreading Love, Peace, Joy and Connection to all corners of the earth and
   most importantly within my own being.

Knowing you are with me always
   and that we shall meet again
Living and loving in that place of both/and

I meet you there and miss you here
In the deepest reveries I both miss you and I feel you

In the most intimate of places I see you
   and long for your physical presence

With all my belief, faith and hope I know you are there
   and see that you have gone

It is in this place of both/and that I both fully live
   and wish to go to where you are

It is from this very vulnerable and precarious position that I open myself up
   to this world, this love, this connection, this joy
and find such peace in retreating from this world,
   such rejuvenation in solitude

Holding you close to me and releasing you to be so free.

I open my heart and there you are, in a face, in a moment, in every country, all over the world, and throughout the Universe.

I open my heart and there you are. So Holy is your Presence.

© Elene Bratton 2/14/2014

This poem was inspired by my service trip to Ramana's Garden in Rishikesh, India, seeing Jamie in every step in every moment. Enjoy!

"God's Heart is different colors, and every color is a country."

—Jamie, 5 years old

~•~

Lessons in Grief

In honor of Ken Druck, master teacher in a grief-illiterate world

If I can admit to myself
that anything of value
could come from the profoundly life anguishing
and life altering grief
that is the loss of a child, that the loss of my child Jamie Morgan
is to me,

If I could admit that, even to myself,
I would talk about the shift from either/or
to both/and
I would no longer convey things as either this or that,
as if that were the only possibility, as if life were that simple,
that succinct
either good or bad
either sad or happy
either pain or joy
either alive or dead
either heartbroken or whole
either shattered or healed
either loved or hated

If I were able to say
that some lesson
some expansion of mind and heart were possible and had

taken place within me from this unspeakable loss

I would talk about the idea of both/and

Always as

both good and bad

both sad and happy

both pain and joy

both alive and dead

both heartbroken and whole

both shattered and healed

both loved and hated,

that this idea of both/and

has been given as a gift to me

given freely from a special man,

who, too, knew the same agonizing journey toward healing,

If I could admit that such a gift could come in the midst of

such an excruciating journey,

Then I would say that the heart-wrenching healing

of such a deep loss

that always continues to take space,

always alive in the vastly dichotomous world of the perpetually bereaved

only exists

where there is only Both/And

And never Either/Or.

© Jamie's Mom, Elene Bratton 1/20/2019

"Poetry is when an emotion has found its thought and the thought has found words."

—Robert Frost

Ode to Initiates

In Sukie Miller's book, "Finding Hope When a Child Dies, What Other Cultures Can Teach Us," she likens a child's death to the initiate ritual in some Native Tribes. They know that parents who lose a child (or children) do not "volunteer" for the loss. They aren't "stronger," or wiser, or more capable of handling the experience; they are simply *forced* into it—whether chosen by fate, chaos, randomness, "life" or however you want to define it: They must walk through the fire. I personally know that the hardest loss for a parent is a child, but equally true, the greatest loss for a young child is a parent. In both situations, those of us left behind are "initiates."

News of death came again on May 27, 2017. Greg Allman died, and, as with most deaths, there's a peculiar twist in that we learn so much more about a person after their passing. But I digress. NPR shared the story of his life as an initiate.

His father was murdered when he was three years old. He grew very close to his big brother, Duane, and together they survived through music as the Allman Brothers Band. After the loss of his brother in a motorcycle crash in 1971, at the age of 24, Greg continued to face his grief every time he played as the Allman Bother's Band, *sin hermano.* (Without his brother.) NPR talked about how his grief influenced his music, but pondered over why he would want to torture himself in that way.

What they didn't understand, as much of our culture doesn't, was *the way of the initiate.* Trial by fire. The way of honoring and remembering, weaving and integrating the loss, the pain, the memory and how, in that way, we also keep the essence of the love and spirit of the loved one alive in us and in the world.

The way of the initiate. So, I say cheers to you Greg, and all the other bravehearts. Those who are willing to be with the depth of the experience, to endure the pain, to get through the fire and blaze a deeper way to be with life in all its brokenness and beauty.

© Elene Bratton 5/27/2017

⌒·⌒

Prompts for the pen of the brokenhearted . . .

Describe your loved one's physical attributes in a haiku . . .

Look to nature and describe your loved one in the clouds, the sway of the tree, the wind, the bright shining sun or moon that lights your way . . .

Write a song, or even a "hook," that describes your love for the person you lost . . .

Make a silly tale of all the things that would annoy you but that you would give anything to experience once again . . .

Write a letter to your loved one . . .

Write a letter to heaven, God, the angels, with Care Instructions for your lost love . . .

Describe a day in the life of the bereaved, and give all the anguished details . . .

Use the letters of your loved one's NAME to create an anagram of their attributes, watermark it with their picture, print and, if you so choose, give to people. (SEE EXAMPLE, right.)

Remember that none of your writing needs to be made public. Share only with a trusted friend when you desire—or share with the world; we need to hear the tales of grief to know we are normal. Everything you do in your grief process is for you to decide if, where, and with whom, to share.

"We need to hear the tales of grief
to know we are normal."

CHAPTER SEVENTEEN

Songs to Grieve By

H ere are some musicians and music we've found comforting, soothing or sometimes helpful in eliciting, articulating and framing feelings of grief. Some of the songs are general and others relate specifically to us.

Music can also be a way to move past the tough outer shell we create in trying to "be strong" for whatever reasons we think we must. Music connects with our life force and moves us deeply. In this way sometimes it helps to facilitate the uncomfortable parts of grief, bypassing the brain and going right into the heart, allowing us to cry, sob, break down and experience the loss.

Don't worry. It won't last forever, but to heal from grief you must go through it, and music can be that tool, even if just in 5-minute increments. Allow yourself to touch the pain and then go back to being strong.

I have listed below the songs that had meaning for us. They could be a starting point to create your own playlist of songs that powerfully resonate with you on your own journey—or your loved ones' play list that brings their presence just a bit closer.

This first list of musicians is comprised of independent (folk/spiritual) artists. Some have their own websites and YouTube channels:

Cidny Bullens—http://www.cidnybullens.com—*Somewhere Between Heaven & Earth*

David Whyte—www.davidwhyte.com—*Poetry A Well Of Grief/News Of Death/Faith*

Don Conoscenti—*Paradox of Grace/The Other Side*

Karl Anthony—www.karlanthony.com—*Hold On to Each Other* (See lyrics below)/*All of Us/Loving Arms/When Will I See You Again?/ Jamie's Joy*

Mark Stanton Welch—www.markstantonwelch.net—*True Balance/I Am A Hero*

Michael Stillwater—www.innerharmony.com—*Graceful Passages*

Scott Kalechstein—www.scottsongs.com—*From the Heart/Touch of Grace/Precious Jamie*

Variety of Artists—http://www.compassionatefriends.org—*Follow the Wind/Songs for the Stained Soul*

These songs are available anywhere music can be heard:

Aimee Mann—*Routine*

Bill Withers/Will Smith—*Just the Two of Us*

Carole King—*You've Got a Friend*

Cat Stevens—*Morning Has Broken*

Doris Day—*Dream a Little Dream of Me*

Eric Clapton—*Tears in Heaven*

Everything But the Girl—*Missing*

Incubus—*Pardon Me*

Jewel—*Pieces of You/Angel/Standing By*

James Taylor—*Fire & Rain/Shower the People/Sweet Baby James*

Josh Groban—*Where You Are*

Mindy Smith—*One Moment More*

Nat King Cole and Natalie Cole—*Unforgettable*

Norah Jones—*Come Away with Me*

Peter, Paul and Mary—*Day is Done*

Police—*Can't Stand Losing You/So Lonely*

REM—*Everybody hurts*

Rod Stewart—*Sailing/I Don't Want to Talk About It*

Sarah McLachlan—*Surfacing/I Will Not Forget You/Wear Your Love Like Heaven/Angel*

Trisha Yearwood—*Inside-out/Melancholy Blue/I Would Have Loved You Anyway*

The White Stripes—*We Are Going to Be Friends*

This list could go on and on. Find songs that bring you closeness, comfort and elicit a good cry. You will know when you hear it if it makes your "Songs to Grieve By" list.

Hold On To Each Other

by *Karl Anthony "AKA Kral Antie"* (how Jamie said his name) *& Jamie*

When the heart hurts . . . there's no place to go
Where your world . . . will seem right
But don't pull back . . . as a matter of fact
Get real close . . . and hold tight
I'm right here . . . and you're over there

but I can still . . . feel your embrace
I'm in your arms . . . as you hold each other
My hand is on your face

So hold on to each other . . . when you can't hold on
Share your tears . . . quiet your fear
And hold on to each other
You're not alone . . . you're closer to home than you think
Please confide . . . in
Someone who loves you . . . and someone you love
We all have pain inside

So hold on to each other . . .

I will call all the angels . . . to help you make it through the nights
You will be surrounded by angels . . . to let you know, I'll be all right
My spirit lives . . . and continues to give I can see . . . through your eyes

I'll be there . . . with whomever you hold

It's beyond . . . the question why

I'm right here . . . and you're over there

But I can still . . . feel your embrace

I'm in your arms . . . as you love each other

Your hand is on my face

I will call all the angels . . . to be with you through the nights

You will be surrounded by angels . . . they will help you hold the light . . .
   hold the light

Hold on to each other . . . Hold on . . . Hold on . . . to each other

"Music is my life. Music runs through my veins. Music
inspires me. Music is a part of me. Music is all around us.
Music soothes me. Music gives me hope when I lose faith.
Music comforts me. Music is my refuge."

—Demi Lovato

grira Sol

CHAPTER EIGHTEEN

Suggested Reading

These are some books we've read thus far. No book is going to solve the problem, but they do help a person to realize that they are not "going crazy" and are not alone. Many of our feelings and pain have been validated by reading about the grief of other parents in our horrible situation.

The Adventures of Caterpillar Jones by J.J. Brothers

This is a great book for pre-teens. There are no pictures, so young children will lose interest, but for pre-teens who are dealing with a grief issue this book will give them comfort and hope. It is a story of a young caterpillar named CJ and his lifelong friend, Sammy. Their story touches on all stages of the life process including facing the death of a loved one, one's own mortality and the possibility of something beyond the body. It is well written, easy to read and has enough tales to let the reader's imagination make its own pictures. It can be enjoyed and discussed as a family.

After Death: How People Around the World Map the Journey After Life, by Sukie Miller, PhD with Suzanne Lipsett

This is an easy-to-read book that has incorporated many beliefs, religions, philosophies and ideas from around the world on what happens when we die. From her research, Ms. Miller gleans four major stages that most cultures' beliefs fit into, although with a wide variety of differences in each stage:

STAGE I—WAITING: Encompasses a range of experiences in which the recently-deceased adjusts (or doesn't adjust) to not having a body.

STAGE II—JUDGMENT: Incorporates many beliefs and ideas about how one's life on earth is accounted for after their life on earth is over.

STAGE III—POSSIBILITIES: Explores what kind of existence varying cultures believe we experience in spirit form.

STAGE IV—RETURN: Explores the belief in reincarnation and the many forms it takes in different cultures throughout the world and the history of humankind. She gives many examples of how she has used the exploration of the afterlife to help those she has worked with who are facing death. She also explores what she calls "vital imagination," which is an experiential altered reality which may be our closest connection to the spirit world.

Although interesting, this book does not touch on the grieving heart. It may be useful for those exploring the philosophy of death and dying. The idea of vital imagination and its hope to connect us to those no longer living in their bodies was promising to us, and that seemed worthwhile to explore.

Against the Dying of the Light: A Father's Journey through Loss
by Leonard Fein

In this exploration of heartbreak and healing, Mr. Fein tries to answer some hard questions, and continue to live, after the death of his 30-year-old daughter. This is one of the most moving accounts we've read on this topic. This was originally a borrowed book but was so engrossing, each page was underlined. The author is able to put into words what is in many bereaved parents' hearts. Dismay, disbelief, how life changes and continues to change over time, and the desire to honor and stay connected are all eloquently discussed. The author writes from his own Jewish perspective, and does not believe in an after-life. Yet he aches to keep his daughter alive and finds ways to do so in the traditions of family. I found it very interesting to learn about traditions of the Jewish faith that help families stay connected to their loved ones.

Andy's Mountain: Fathers Grieve Too by Dwight L. Patton

A father's brief account of his 17-year-old's illness and death from cancer. This author focuses much of the book on his inability to face the seriousness of his son's condition and of the grief process. He did not allow himself to grieve much until 10 years after the event when he found Compassionate Friends. He talks extensively about the lonely path many men take in this situation and how he especially reaches out to those who believe they don't need support. Each chapter is short but full of experiences most grieving parents can relate to. In addition, he outlines many of the tools available to help people in grief including counseling, group support, books and the internet. It is easy-reading and especially good for those who feel they have to go it alone.

Awakening from Grief: Finding the Way Back to Joy
by John E. Welshons

In this book, author John Welshons speaks from his personal experience and work with those who are dying. He touches on all types of loss. His ideas give the reader permission to grieve and to be present with those who are dying. It is a generalist approach, so if you need to hear only about your situation, you may not be satisfied. I think it is good to read after you have been along the "yoga of loss" journey for a while and can appreciate his advice.

It is a great book for professionals who want a better insight into working with grieving and dying people. "The gifts we give ourselves" chapter is full of ways to be in grief that allow for expression and reawakening to life. It is sensitively written with many heartwarming stories.

The Bereaved Parent by Harriet Sarnoff Schiff

This is a good book for understanding the impact of the death of a child on the family. It can help those on the outside to understand the complex experience of this type of loss.

Book of Meditations by Sister Wendy

A beautiful collection of photos and simple, thoughtful meditations on life that create a personal and visual journey into your own soul. It is warm, inspirational and deeply moving in a very subtle way.

A Broken Heart Still Beats: After Your Child Dies
by Anne McCracken & Mary Semel

This is a compilation of personal stories from famous people and literature (movies and books) that deal with varying aspects of the death of a child or children. Both authors lost a child. Neither believes in a spiritual afterlife or the presence of God. Their research of this literature offers a different perspective than that of a spiritual or religious view. A social worker and a journalist, the authors are very sensitive, compassionate and articulate in their descriptions of the impact of this type of loss.

Finding Hope When a Child Dies: What Other Cultures Can Teach Us by Sukie Miller, PhD with Doris Ober

While this book offers no first-hand personal experience (the author has not lost a child), it offers a wealth of information for those seeking to be able to view their circumstance from perspectives outside of mainstream American culture. The author begins by talking about the thing those who have lost children know: We have no language with which to describe our experience. She then offers an overview of other cultures' takes on the death of a child. You may not agree with these new views, but having them opens up your own ability to know there is no one way to what it is. You can then feel free to believe in what brings you the most comfort and solace. She also talks about the bereaved parents as "initiates" in the ancient use of the word. She describes the eight themes of initiation and likens them to the journey of the bereaved parent.

A Grief Observed by C.S. Lewis

The account of a grieving husband, the descriptions used to chronicle his experience are brilliant and real. Even though he did not lose a child (rather, he lost the love of his life, as he had no children), the loss hit him very hard. He is able to describe his experience in a way only an artist can, with depth and breadth. He kept a journal from the early days of his loss, so his emotions are raw and unfiltered.

A Grief Unveiled: One Father's Journey Through the Death of a Child
by Gregory Floyd

This is a father's account of the sudden death of his six-and-a-half-year-old son and the family's first two years of grief. He has a strong Catholic faith, which he leans on, and talks about it intensively throughout the book. His faith does not offset his pain, but serves as a backdrop to his experience. This book reveals how the family survived together and was able to continue the memory of their son, John Paul, so that he stayed an important part of their lives. He talks about how his marriage was affected and how it was also a source of comfort and strength. This is a great account of the strength of family in times of crisis.

The Grieving Time: A Year's Account of Recovery from Loss
by Anne M. Brooks

This is an account of a deeply grieving widow over twelve months of her loss. She writes it from month-to-month as a diary of her thoughts, feelings and experiences. Her description of grief is real and timeless for anyone who has lost someone very near. She talks about things rarely expressed in any "how-to" book on grief. For example, how the paradox of knowing that you have the option of suicide helps you to live through the darkest times of grief. It is a raw account of bereavement and how we heal, in time, whether we want to or not.

Hannah's Gift: Lessons from a Life Fully Lived by Maria Housden

A mother's account of life with her daughter and family, during her daughter's illness and last year of life. Housden's ability to capture the thoughts and feelings of grief are powerful. After a year she wonders if her daughter could come back. "It would only be fair since we have suffered all this time without her." It is a good book for anyone whose child was ill prior to passing. It is told in story form, in short bursts, so it is easier to take for the newly-bereaved whose attention span is short due to the trauma.

Healing After Loss: Daily Meditations for Working Through Grief
by Martha Whitmore Hickman

This book can be used on a daily basis to focus on some aspect of grief. It can be used year after year. It offers quotes and reflections along with an affirmation that can be used throughout the day.

Inside Grief: An Anthology on Death, Loss and Bereavement
by Line Wise

A book of poetry on death, dying and grief. It is a very personal book written by those affected. It is divided into sections to reflect writings on a variety of topics that describe the questions of life: "Who Am I?" "What is life all about?" "Why am I here in this world?" Anyone who has faced a serious loss or life issue will appreciate the poetry in this book.

The Lessons of Love by Melody Beattie

This book is written out of her own experience of the loss of her only son in a ski accident when he was 13 years old. It is the story of the healing of her life and that of her daughters who had taken him skiing. She focuses on her healing journey after the death and her eventual ability to reclaim a life she had fought hard to establish for herself and her children as a single parent. She confronts her beliefs, God and, ultimately, herself to be able to rejoin life, even when crushed by it.

The Lord is My Shepherd: Healing Wisdom of the Twenty-third Psalm by Harold S. Kushner

The book takes a classic bible verse that is an old favorite for many in their time of need. It is used at many services to honor those who have passed but serves as comfort and support for those who are grieving the loss. This book takes each line in the verse and talks about its practical and religious applications. He gives perspective from various religions. The psalm is discussed in the context of both its historical perspective and the modern day practical application. The author illuminates the life lessons that are contained within the grace of the psalm. The book is very interesting, but unlike Rabbi Kushner's famous writing, "When Bad Things Happen" (detailed below), this book feels more religious. Although he apologizes for using the male reference to God, the use of "he" gives a distinctly humanlike quality to God—a God with a will for us, doing things to us or for us, or being by our side. For those with strong convictions, this book will probably give a lot of insight into an age old psalm. For those just wanting comfort, I found it fell short of earlier works.

The Lovely Bones by Alice Sebold

Written as a fictional book from the perspective of a murdered 14-year-old girl after her death, this book gives some hope even in its heaviness of what "heaven" may be like and the chance that we really do stay connected. In the book, the main character Susie Salmon shares with us her attempts and successes at reaching her family, trying to help them solve her murder and how family members, friends, even the detective, are touched by her life and haunted by her death. The depictions of grief are real and the traumatic effect on the family is believable. You also feel the sadness of this young spirit who continues to long for her life on earth and how she tries to keep on living through others. It is the type of book that is hard to put down. Very well written and almost poetic.

Many Lives, Many Masters by Brian Weiss

This book describes the author's journey while counseling a client. He attempts to hypnotize her in order to regress her to early childhood to find out why she has so many fears and phobias. She easily goes back even beyond childhood into many of her previous incarnations. Brian Weiss apparently didn't believe in any of this reincarnation stuff before he got together with this client. By the second or third chapter, however, he's convinced. There are just too many details for this client to have made it all up. There is some kind of comfort believing we have seen and will see our loved ones many times. And then, it doesn't mean all is okay. Most of our grief seems to stem from losing our loved one in this incarnation. It is interesting to study what we can learn about where our loved one has gone, though, and it does help for those of us who lose faith, or never had much faith to begin with, to know they are still around.

The Spiritual Lives of Bereaved Parents by Dennis Klass

(Note: I do not recommend reading this until after two years into grieving. —Elene)

Although not written by a bereaved parent, Dennis Klass has spent decades immersing himself in the extremely sad world of those who have lost a child. He admits that he cannot, and as a parent does not want to, fully understand the feelings of parents who have lost children. He has, however, had the openness of heart and the courage to sit with bereaved parents and hold a space for them. He does not define spirituality in its typical religious manner but opens the meaning to embrace the journey of pain, redefining life and the quest to stay connected to our children who are no longer in their bodies. He has had the courage to really look at the experience of bereaved parents and put words and concepts to that experience.

Reading the book helped us make sense of why we do so much to keep Jamie alive. It validated our efforts. It also gives direction to those who have thus far suffered in silence. Although everyone grieves differently, the words of this book inspire all bereaved parents (and people) to honor their process and their loved one. It describes for the reader what is happening on a spiritual level much as other books describe what is happening on a psychological level.

I recommend this book to all clergy and other helping professionals so they can better understand the depth of the bereaved's journey and help those they work with to understand their own process of grief.

The reason I do not recommend this book to those with less than two years "out" from the loss of their child is because, while everyone's process is different, certain books were painful for me initially as they told me about how I was feeling, reacting, thinking—like a kind of education on what this grief might be like for ME, personally, in real time. And although it was helpful to not feel like something was wrong with my reactions, it was just too close to home. I had not yet built up a protective coating from the pain and shock. I was just free falling through the experience and had not yet formed my own perspective of what was happening.

On the other hand, reading stories about others' grief gave me little crumbs of relating to their feelings, but it wasn't so harsh, so hard to swallow. It went down a little easier.

It's already hard, rough, excruciating enough. This is why I recommend letting a little psychology "skin" grow back before peeling back that curtain through books like **The Spiritual Lives of Bereaved Parents.**

A Time to Grieve: Meditations for Healing After the Death of a Loved One by Carol Staudacher

A reflective reading and message for varying aspects of grief. She has an index that allows the reader to find the specific topic to reflect on. She describes it this way (paraphrased): *Thinking your way through grief doesn't work. Grief is a release process, a discovery process, a healing process. We cannot use our minds alone. The brain must follow the heart at a respectful distance. It is our hearts that ache when a loved one dies. The heart will blaze the trail through the thickest of grief.*

When Bad Things Happen to Good People by Harold S. Kushner

This book presents an overview of commonly-held beliefs about tragic events, and an argument against most of these ideas. A Rabbi, Kushner gives a faith-filled and sensitive account of the role God plays in life's tragedies. Many of us ask the question, "How could God let this happen to me?" Kushner offers help in answering this question and others, opening new views and helpful ways to approach those facing crisis. The author lost his young son to the rare disease "progeria" (rapid aging).

When the Bough Breaks by Judith R. Bernstein, Ph.D.

Confronted with the ugliest of life's experiences, the death of her 25-year-old son after a 16-month battle with illness, the author/doctor and her doctor-husband did what they knew: They began a research project. They set out to find how parents survive the wrath of such a great grief. They wanted to know how parents fared over time. How did they get through the years living with loss, having that loss as a back-drop. They interviewed dozens of parents from Compassionate Friends who were at least five years away from the tragedy. She identifies the ways in which the person's life is altered and values changed forever. She also talks about what is helpful (and not) from friends, family, and clergy, making this a good "how to" book for those who love or want to help someone in deep grief.

The Worst Loss: How Families Heal from the Death of a Child
by Barbara Rosoff

A practical guide to understanding how the loss of a child affects the family. Rosoff reviews various ways children die and gives specific information on how families may feel and how they may deal with each type of loss based on the circumstances under which the loved one passed away. She also reviews a history of losing children throughout the ages and how our expectations have changed about the likelihood of experiencing this type of loss. The author has not lost a child but interviews dozens of families who have. We gave copies to some very close family members early on and it really helped them to understand more about what we were going through.

Prayer to my Guardian Angel

Dear Guardian Angel,
Thank you for staying close and protecting me
Thank you for helping me make the right decisions
Thank you for helping me to be loving
Thank you for showing me the ways to be happy
and to make other people happy
Thank you for loving me so much.

Amen

"On the death of a friend, we should consider
that the fates through confidence have devolved
on us the task of a double living, that we have
henceforth to fulfill the promise of our friend's
life also, in our own, to the world."
—Henry David Thoreau

*We came across this quote and it resonated deeply within us,
solidifying the idea that we would carry on Jamie's life through his legacy,
which was very clear by how he always moved in the world with Love, Joy,
Peace and Connecting to everything and everyone around him.*

Because his
work isn't
done and
his love still
exists

After we arrived at the hospital and they let us out of the family waiting room to go see him, when we saw him on life support, I felt our Jamie was already gone. Without thought, and from a guttural but knowing place, I simply blurted out: "He's Not Here."

The doctors had told us in that room that his brain had been deprived of oxygen for over forty minutes, but until I saw him with my own eyes, I had hope. And because they put him on machines, the doctors were now asking us to decide whether to keep him on life support or let him go. We decided to let him go, because we knew that the same angel that had given him to us had already scooped up his Spirit. But that decision was not ours to make; his body shut down on its own and he officially left it at 10 P.M. on April 24, 2002.

As quickly and unexpectedly as he had arrived, he was gone, leaving us with our descent into Hell.

To say we were in total shock can't describe it, but at the same moment, we felt Jamie's spirit of giving begin to guide us. A woman approached us and asked if we would consider donating Jamie's organs. Only his corneas and heart valves could be useful, but we didn't hesitate, and we said "yes." We didn't know it then, but this was the first act of Jamie's Joy. From that moment Jamie has continued to give as he had been so willing to do in life.

Jamie's service was a celebration of his life and an honoring of our grief. Instead of friends and family sending flowers, we initially suggested that they give donations to organizations that helped people. What do you do with money received from the death of your child? It felt perverse, but we took comfort that it could help someone else. I know not all families are in this position; some need these vital resources to help with expenses or to survive, but for us it was difficult to accept, unless we could use the donations to preserve a legacy for Jamie. Then the idea was given to us (from Jamie) to save the donations and determine later where the money would be donated. This took a lot of pressure off an already intense moment.

Our minister, Blair Tabor, from Christ Church Unity, agreed to hold the donations at the church. That was the start of "Jamie's Joy." Since that time, we have transferred the funds to San Diego Foundation, a non-profit organization. That has allowed for the creation of the "Jamie's Joy Memorial Fund" to honor his life and memory. It is described as such: "Elene and Mychael established the Jamie's Joy Fund in loving memory of their five-year-old son, Jamie. The fund seeks to enrich the lives of all living beings by supporting activities and organizations that promote Love, Joy, Peace & Connections—attributes expressing the best of Jamie."

Every year around his birthday we give to other non-profit groups that help kids, youth, and families focusing on the ages Jamie would have been. We've given to organizations all over the world (see list of recipients, below). Every year we focus on agencies and organizations that exemplify Jamie's Joy by asking, "Would Jamie like it?" "WWJD— What Would Jamie Do?" and, "Does this work exemplify the qualities of LOVE*JOY*PEACE*CONNECTION?"

Annually, Jamie's Joy sponsors a child somewhere in the world with the basics: food, clothing and shelter, in addition to grief programs through the Compassionate Friends and Rady's Children's Hospital among others. We host a website with grief support and resources to help people who have had loss. We have also made space for people to share their stories about Jamie and we have shared our process of grief and healing through our writings, book reviews and music suggestions to help others under- stand and assuage grief are also listed on the website.

But Jamie's Joy is more than a charity fund or a website to honor and remember Jamie, or an attempt to educate our society on how to sup- port those facing the deepest of human emotions as "the bereaved." We attempt to live this legacy in many facets of our lives. In the early days we attended life-sharing luncheons, participated in a San Diego County program entitled, "Traffic Victims' Remembrance

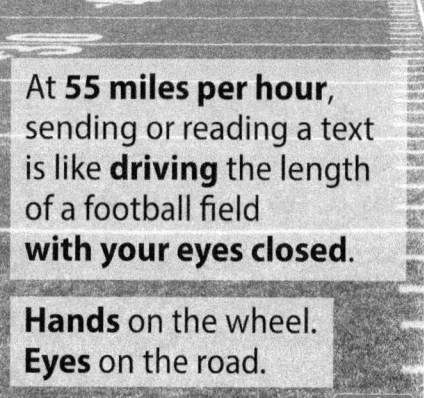

At **55 miles per hour**, sending or reading a text is like **driving** the length of a football field **with your eyes closed**.

Hands on the wheel. **Eyes** on the road.

www.cdc.gov

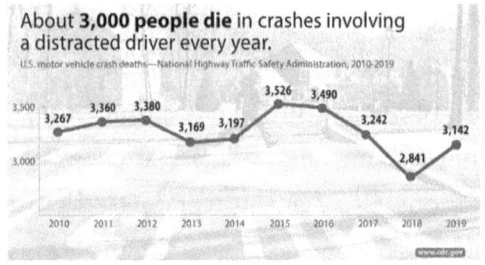

About **3,000 people die** in crashes involving a distracted driver every year.

U.S. motor vehicle crash deaths—National Highway Traffic Safety Administration, 2010-2019

Day," developed and offered the workshop "Honoring and Remembering" to help families with alternate ways to navigate the passing of loved ones who have crossed over and to honor the grief process. We've built houses in Tijuana, Mexico, given dozens of interviews to highlight the gravity of distracted driving by giving a face to the tragedy, hosted an annual clean up, beautification and butterfly release every Saturday prior to Memorial Day in our neighborhood at Jamie's Park, worked at the Interfaith shelter to sponsor and volunteer for their annual homeless shelter program.

We continue to host an annual clean up and work with Interfaith Shelter Network, and our current focus, in addition to local service projects, is to sponsor service travel, where we can spread Jamie's legacy through the world. We just made our long-awaited second trip to Ramana's Garden Orphanage in Rishikesh, India in the fall of 2023, staying six days at Ramana's Garden and bringing Jamie's Joy to kids who have been there since our last visit nine

years ago, who remembered us, as well as many new faces who got to know Jamie's love through our hands and hearts. I envision going to many other countries, traveling throughout the continental United States, and staying right in our own back yards, providing service, Jamie's Joy style.

As much as we have done outwardly, Jamie's Joy has been an avenue for each member of our family and extended friendship family to heal their own grief, whatever that may be, and to continue a path of healing by following Jamie's life and legacy in their own ways. As we share our grief and continue to talk about Jamie, people share their stories of loss and let us know how Jamie touched their lives while he was in his body and since he has been a spirit among us. Jamie has also been an inspiration to those who did not know him in his body, but who have found inspiration in his life and legacy and in our response to this loss. Some that never met Jamie "in life" felt his presence just from seeing his photo and count him among their angels.

We've also been recipients of much compassion and support. People have been so respectful of our human process of grief. One of the most helpful responses is to sit and listen, to be "there or present" for us, even when the grief has been so intense that it felt un-survivable. For those who can, this is a most precious gift. When we can bear the unbearable with another, when we allow them to say and feel whatever they need to in order to get through the moment, even if they face that same moment time and time again, we are a living, healing balm by being present.

Just as a cut needs air and sunshine, grief needs a witness to heal. Allowing the bereaved to teach you what will be helpful for them provides the safety in which heal. Judging another's process, however well intentioned, often delays healing as the bereaved becomes more isolated. I know in this quick-fix, silver-lining society, even well-meaning remarks can feel like judgment. Remember that whatever you are feeling, the persons closest to the loss are feeling it on a level indescribable and hard to hold. Holding it is a great gift. Don't try to fix feelings or "make them feel better," because they're not going to feel better for quite a while, and some things and days will always remain a tender part of the human grief experience.

For us, we shaped this human experience into part of our spiritual life by honoring Jamie as a continuing spiritual presence. This way seems very befitting of the person that he was. Of course, there's always the human part of us—that longing and sadness we feel for him. Remembering the profound and deep things that Jamie said at such a tender young age helps us to recognize that continuation of the relationship. I said early on that I will continue my relationship with my son, even if he doesn't have a body. Nobody can take that from me. We believe Jamie knew God and was connected to Spirit in a way that many people may never experience. This was evidenced by his response, "Cuz, God made me that way." Jamie knew his source, his value, his connection. He knew that "all the world is in God's heart and that we are all part of God's heart." Knowing this, knowing we eternally "Inter-are," always connected through eternity, that life is eternal, and death is immortal, brings us comfort (on most days— but not always), even through our anguished tears.

To learn more about Jamie's Joy, please visit www.jamiesjoy.org. (Jamie's Joy is an all-volunteer organization. 100% of your donations and all proceeds from this book go towards helping kids and families in need.)

Recipients of Jamie's Joy Memorial Fund Grants (Alpha order)

Augustinian Scholarship Fund A Su Futuro "who provides disadvantaged students access to education and support for academic success so that they can create a promising future for themselves and for the community in which they live."

*Compassionate Friends provides support nationally and locally to families who have lost a child at any age, from any cause. www.compassionatefriends.org

Canyon Lands helps maintain the biodiversity of our San Diego canyons, restoring waterways, leading to ocean health. www.SDcanyonlands.org

*Rady's Children Hospital is the hospital where Jamie was cared for at his time of transition. Jamie's Joy sponsored a concert featuring Karl and Jeanne Anthony (www.karlanthony.com) for the inpatient children and another concert for bereaved families and the public at the hospital (www.chsd.org). Jamie's grandmother Fran DeVoss's "CD of Lullabies" was also given to the kids at Children's Hospital.

(The) I Am Foundation donates books to organizations and people who can't afford them. Jamie's Joy sponsored children's books and CD's to Language

* Denotes annual giving.

Academy (Jamie's Spanish/French/English immersion school), which received English/Spanish versions of "Aesock's Travels" by Gretchen McMasters. "Yo Soy" by Edel Rodriguez was distributed to the entire 4th grade class at the Language Academy. 50 copies of "I Am" by Steve Viglione (affirmational children's book) were given to Unity Kid's Camp. "CD of Lullabies" by Fran DeVoss (Jamie's Grandma) was given to every SD County Head Start. www.iamfoundation.org

---

I Love a Clean San Diego raises awareness and helps build a recycling culture to protect our environment. www.IlovecleanSD.org

---

It's Just For Kids is an organization that sponsors volunteer groups to go to Cuba and build playgrounds. Elene went in 2005, building playgrounds and very much felt Jamie's presence. www.itsjustthekids.org

---

Jenna Druck Foundation Children's Program based in San Diego is a foundation that provided a variety of no-cost bereavement services to help families after the death of a child. (Closed in 2013.) www.jennadruck.org

---

Kid's Camp sponsors children to attend a local summer camp through **Unity Church**. www.unitysandiego.org

---

Life Sharing was the first giving Jamie made. He gave his corneas and heart valves, inspiring us to continue his legacy. www.lifesharing.org

---

Monarch School provides an education to K-12 students whose families are undomiciled. Helping provide education and hope for children and their families. www.monarchschools.org

---

Ocean Conservancy protects national and international oceans from pollution, climate change and other man made problems, preserving species, doing research and educating the next generation of scientists. www.oceanconservancy.com

---

Ocean Discovery Institute is a "living lab" for kids from City Heights to learn about ocean health and species conservation.

Parent's Circle Families Forum consists of bereaved families of the Israeli-Palestinian conflict who are supporting peace, reconciliation and tolerance through providing support to Israeli and Palestinian families as well as campaigning for a peace agreement that will resolve the conflict and open a new chapter in Israeli-Palestinian relations. www.theparentscircle.com

---

Ramana's Garden takes care of all ages of children in India who become orphaned due to abuse, domestic violence, disability and many forms of poverty. They raise food in their organic garden, and educate all children to the 8th grade-level. Additionally they provide a loving, caring, nurturing home to all who come there. www.ramanas.org

---

Reality Changers is an organization that helps low income, under achieving students to become the 1st in their family to attend college. www.realitychangers.org

---

Responsibility is an organization founded by David Lynch, who has been providing an education to the children of Tijuana. Located on the site of a dump where the students reside, the school affords the only local educational opportunity these children will have. In 2002, Jamie's Joy made its first monetary donation. It supported a 5-year-old to attend kindergarten. www.responsibilityonline.org

---

*Save the Children Foundation sponsors a child by providing for their basic needs for one year. www.savethechildren.org

---

Smile Train In the spirit of Jamie's infectious smile, Smile Train was granted for the opportunity they give children around the world born with cleft palates to also have a wonderful smile. Besides bringing a smile to their faces, the surgery performed also can help them regain the ability to eat and speak properly. www.smiletrain.org

---

The Somali-Bantu Association serves a minority culture within the Somalian community in San Diego. They have both mentoring programs to help children and teens achieve their educational goals, as well as a soccer team allowing the youth to acculturate into the broader community through league sports. www.sbaoa.org

---

Tariq Khamisa Foundation is a locally-based (San Diego) foundation established in memory of Tariq Khamisa, slain in 1995 by Tony Hicks. Founded by Tariq's father and Tony's grandfather, the organization provides educational violence prevention programs and services to youth nationwide. www.tkf.org 1-888-help-tkf

---

TransenDance is a San Diego dance troupe that serves low-income, inner city children to reach their full potential through the arts. http://www.tdarts.org

---

Urban Street Angels (USA) works with homeless transitional-age youth by providing basic needs of shelter and helping them find a positive forward direction. www.urbanStreetAngels.org

(The) Youth Advisory Board promotes a program called "4 or 40" based on the Emmy-winning short film centered on the hard life choices made daily by teens. The idea, conceived by the District Attorney's Youth Advisory Board, is to have youth speak out on the issues they face by visiting classrooms to screen the film and speak on its message. www.choose4or40.com

— Photos by JGElias

Photos by JGElias

© Amazing Memories Pho

ABOUT THE AUTHOR

I have always been an activist and an original thinker, just like my parents. I am one of the only two in my family to graduate from college, the other being my maternal grandmother, who went back to school in her 50's, in the 1950's, after raising three kids. During my college days, I started an Alliance for Survival chapter—an early effort at environmental justice that continues to this day. I am a bi-racial **Black** woman of color, for whom the journey to feel comfortable in my skin was long and rough.

As a mother of five children (two living) and five grandchildren (four living), I have had multiple losses—two children before their birth, and my granddaughter at 8 years old in 2008, along with both of my parents before the age of 30. My father was murdered, and my life has been marred by grief since I was about 10 years old. All those losses, as hard and painful as they felt, couldn't prepare me for "the worst loss": that of my son Jamie in 2002.

Losing Jamie reshaped and redefined my life. It has brought an unrelenting depth of pain and a deepened compassion, developing my relationship to those without their bodies in profound ways that has allowed me to less fearfully, more loudly and fully, live intertwining their legacies into the tapestry of my own life—an honoring and remembering, rather than a letting go and "forgetting."

My passion is being of service to humans, animals and the earth by honoring the deepest in me through love, peace, joy and connection; by practicing selfcare, healing, connection and service. This helps me be better in all of my roles—mother, sister, grandmother, friend and therapist—among others. I have dedicated my work life to serving the most underserved in our community by working in public behavioral health (mental health/substance use) in a variety of settings from jails and hospitals to substance recovery programs, juvenile treatment centers, outpatient clinics and case-management. In my private practice, I offer therapy, workshops, retreats and healing ceremonies for those experiencing losses and familial distress due to a history of trauma. I also perform personalized marriage ceremonies for people of all faiths and beliefs (or none at all).

My work (personal and professional) focuses on healing the wounds and holes that come along life's path to create room for Spiritual connection through therapy, intensives, workshops and retreats that allow people the time and space they need to slow down, reflect, breathe, (re)connect and heal.

When my own heart was broken, I found my way back to life through service by co-founding (with Jamie's dad) a non-profit we named Jamie's Joy after our beloved son to continue his legacy of Love*Joy*Peace* Connection. I am also a poet, essayist and author.

Lastly, and firstly, I am a divinely made human, here to practice healing for myself, others and the planet through sharing my passion, compassion, love and authenticity in order to continually grow into who I was born to be.

It is my truest desire that by sharing my personal experience, strength and hope in these pages, you will be deeply moved to find your own winding road to recovery, whatever your own life story has been.

Elene Bratton, M.S., LMFT
Jamie's Mom &
Cofounder, Jamie's Joy

POSTSCRIPT

While finalizing this manuscript in the summer of 2022, Jamie's Joy received the following email:

-------- Original message --------
From: Mychael McNeeley <███████████████████████>
Date: 8/2/22 8:52 PM (GMT-08:00)
To: Elene Bratton <███████████████████>
Subject: Note from Jamie's Joy

This is addressed to Jamie's family. I hope this message finds you well. I've been trying to find the words to write to you all day and have been going back and forth with myself wondering if contacting you was the right thing to do. But I trust with everything in my heart that it is. My name is Jaelyn. I went to Language Academy and was in the French program. I know this is out of the blue . . . but it's not random by any means. I never met your son personally, however we are the same age and he would've been most likely in my grade.

I have a very vague memory of attending his memorial in the auditorium and being there when your family planted his beautiful memorial tree outside of my classroom. Since that day I have had reoccurring dreams spread out over the last 20 years of being in that small courtyard where the tree is planted. I never understood why I dreamt of that location and could remember those dreams, as that space did not have a significant connection for me. But it's always been one of those dreams I can't seem to forget. Although I don't recall ever seeing Jamie in those dreams, I always felt a sense of purpose and connection that I could not understand . . . until last night.

I have been spiritually connected and gifted with psychic sense and mediumship my whole life. My boyfriend and sister and I just came back from Sedona this last weekend and it seemed to have re-awakened a connection. Last night just before falling totally asleep, I had a spiritual knock on my door. I was consumed with a mental image of the grass patch area where Jamie's tree is planted. I felt like I had just entered that same reoccurring dream I've had over the years except this time I was awake and conscious. A beautiful little boy with gorgeous brown curls about 6 years old or so appeared. I had a feeling it was the little boy that had the tree planted for him. He knew my name and had told me he has been trying to reach me for many years now. He said there was a spiritual connection that we shared even though we had never met before. I asked the boy his name and he told me it was Jamie. He told me at the time of his passing, I was an individual he could easily connect with due to my spiritual awareness and our connectedness from being at the same school.

He said he had tried over the years to visit me in my dreams, which explains the reoccurring dream of the tree and being in that area. I just was too young to understand that someone was trying to deliver me a message. He was so happy to be able to finally connect and he asked me to deliver a message to his family. I felt very nervous at first to reach out since I wasn't sure if I would even find a way to contact you or if what I was experiencing was just my imagination or sleep deprivation.

I told him I was a little scared to deliver a message to a family 20 years after passing for fear I may open old wounds or cause any distress or anxiety. He told me not to worry, I would find a way to connect with you and you would be more open to hearing this than I thought. Since I had never met Jamie in person and had no recollection of his name prior to last night, I took a shot in the dark. All day today at work, I've been searching the internet for any information on a boy named Jamie who went to (sic) language academy, news articles, Facebook anything . . . I was going to resort to contacting some of my old teachers to see if they had any information to share . . . and right before giving up I found this page.

As soon as I saw his picture when the webpage loaded I burst into tears. The little boy in the picture was the exact boy I saw last night. I've been so overwhelmed all day and knew that it truly was Jamie that came to visit me. He wanted me to express to you that he sees the pain and suffering you are experiencing to this day. He said he is worried that his family is holding onto guilt that is not meant to be with them. He wants you to know he is with you and wants you to be able to keep moving forward in happiness. It's all he wants for the people he loves the most.

While I was writing this message, Jamie channeled me and wanted to relay this message to you . . .

"mommy daddy, let go of your hurt and fear. It's time not to be scared anymore and to live life and enjoy the beauty of the physical world. i'm with my angels and everything here feels like love. it's warm and bright and the ocean here is never cold. Im not sad and i dont feel like im missing out on anything that I wouldve had in my physical life. Its fun here. but i dont want to see my family sad. go to the beach please and meet me there. when you go to the water, walk in it. when you see the spot in the ocean that looks sparklier than all the rest and the water starts to feel warm thats how youll know ill be there. You have spent all these years living your lives for me and now at the earthly age of 25 I want you to live it for you. I can take care of everything I need to. You did the best job any parents ever could. i love you with everything in my heart."

I understand this may be overwhelming but I couldn't ignore his request and I feel a responsibility to share his words and message to you. I know we have never met but I feel so much love for Jamie and your family. Please reach out to me if you ever want to. I'd be happy to talk to you or meet. My phone number is 619-███████.

I truly hope this message finds you and I know with Jamie's guidance, it will. Love, Jaelyn.

PRAISE

"Jamie's Joy – Celebrating life, Creating Legacy, Honoring Grief is a beautiful expression of feeling your life, and not allowing the worst possible pain to obscure your potential to be able to live again. It was an honor to have known Jamie, and is a blessing to see and feel his light continue to shine so bright."

—KARL ANTHONY, Musician

"Elene's masterpiece, Jamie's Joy – Celebrating life, Creating Legacy, Honoring Grief is a brilliant treatise on how a tragedy can be transformed for the good of society with a clear call of action to strengthen one's emotional resilience to positively navigate life's toughest challenges. This book is a gift to anyone in need of healing and solace. My prayer is that it finds its way to every heavy heart."

—AZIM N. KHAMISA, ANK Enterprises, Inc, Founder & CEO

"I remember Jamie fondly. He was one very playful angel in human form. He was irresistible, and I, like many others, was drawn into his aura of joy and couldn't help but join in on the fun he was always having. Being friends with Mychael and Elene, I witnessed their deepest of pain. Having had my own child since, I understand a little bit better the devastation that they went through. This book is a testimony to Elene's ongoing love for her child, no matter his form. It is also a love letter for anyone who has suffered this kind of tragedy. Elene has used this experience as a doorway to deep healing through supporting others in crises, and this book is an extension of her service. Through her heartfelt sharing of her experience, tears, and triumphs, your heart will find strength. Jamie was an angel, and now, though her devotion to serving others, so is Elene. This is how we can find and create meaning in a meaningless tragedy. Drink deeply of what is offered here, and you will feel comforted and less alone, because you are not."

—SCOTT GRACE, author of *Teach Me How to Love*

"Jamie's Joy is a captivating story of a mother's journey through profound loss and grief. But it is so much more. Jamie's spirit infuses this book with heartfelt wisdom that will help you celebrate life, love, innocence, and goodness."

——BARRY VISSELL, MD AND JOYCE VISSELL, RN, MS, authors of *The Shared Heart and Models of Love.*

For More Resources Visit: JamiesJoy.org
or contact the author at jamiesjoy.org@gmail.com

www.ingramcontent.com/pod-product-compliance
Lightning Source LLC
Chambersburg PA
CBHW071155130626
46553CB00004B/1667